Presented to:

Ken & Kristi Vellalpand

From:

Graceland Community Church

Date:

June 15, 2002

On Your First Child's dedication

God's Little Lessons
for Parents

Honor Books
Tulsa, Oklahoma

God's Little Lessons for Parents
ISBN 1-56292-997-6
Copyright © 2001 by Honor Books
P.O. Box 55388
Tulsa, Oklahoma 74155

Introduction

Parenting is one of the most challenging jobs
any of us will ever tackle. And it's one for which
there is little or no formal training. So what's a
parent to do?

The good news is that God's Word is filled with
the instruction and encouragement we parents need
to face our most daunting responsibility with
confidence. It offers advice on topics as diverse as
anger and forgiveness, sorrow and joy, discipline
and patience, faith and fear. The Bible contains all
you will ever need to be a successful parent.

That's why we have included so much Scripture
in this helpful little book. But *God's Little Lessons
for Parents* is more than a book of verses. It also
provides a powerful devotional story to help you
live out each day. We pray that as you read through
its pages, you will discover all that God has for you
as a person and as a parent.

Table of Contents

Anger

Wherefore, my beloved brethren, let every man be swift to hear, slow to speak, slow to wrath: For the wrath of man worketh not the righteousness of God.

James 1:19-20 KJV

8

A gentle answer turns away wrath, but a harsh word stirs up anger.

Proverbs 15:1

You yourselves are to put off all these: anger, wrath, malice, blasphemy, filthy language out of your mouth.

Colossians 3:8 NKJV

Cease from anger, and forsake wrath: fret not thyself in any wise to do evil.

Psalm 37:8 KJV

Crying over Spilled Eggs

A mother remembers one summer day when her nine-year-old son and a friend were getting a bottle of juice from the refrigerator. She had spent hours that morning scrubbing, waxing, and polishing the kitchen floor, so she cautioned the boys not to spill anything. They tried so hard to be careful that they accidentally bumped a tray of eggs on the door shelf, splattering eggs all over her clean floor.

The boys' eyes widened with alarm as she exploded angrily. "Get out of here—now!" she shouted as they headed for the door.

9

By the time she had finished cleaning up the mess, she had calmed down. To make amends, she set a tray of cookies on the table along with the juice and some glasses. But when she called the boys, there was no answer. They had gone somewhere else to play, someplace where her angry voice couldn't reach them.

Sometimes we forget how devastating our angry words can be to a child. Anger separates us from those we love. It shatters that intimate relationship that all of us desire to share with our families. Ask for God's help in keeping your anger under control.[1]

Anger

An angry man stirs up strife, And a hot-tempered man abounds in transgression.

Proverbs 29:22 NASB

10

Do not associate with one easily angered, or you may learn his ways and get yourself ensnared.

Proverbs 22:24-25

He that is slow to anger is better than the mighty; and he that ruleth his spirit than he that taketh a city.

Proverbs 16:32 KJV

If you stay calm, you are wise, but if you have a hot temper, you only show how stupid you are.

Proverbs 14:29 TEV

Hammering on Others

One of the most common expressions used to describe losing your temper is to "fly off the handle." This phrase refers to the head of a hammer coming loose from its handle as the carpenter attempts to use it. Several things can happen as a result:

First, the hammer becomes useless—no longer good for work. When you lose your temper, you often lose your effectiveness. Anything you say may not be taken seriously and is likely to be unproductive.

Second, the hammerhead—twirling out of control—is likely to cause some type of damage to anything in its path. When you lose your temper, you cause damage even if you don't realize it—perhaps physically to people or objects in your way, and nearly always emotionally to those who feel they are the victims of this uncontrolled wrath.

Third, the repair of both the hammer and the resulting damage takes time. When you lose your temper, you may recover quickly, but the victim of a hot temper rarely recovers as quickly.

So, as you can see, losing your temper with your children because you're angry is not the best way to handle conflict in life. Keep your temper today. Your children do not want it.

Assurance

As far as the east is from the west, So far has He removed our transgressions from us.

Psalm 103:12 NKJV

12

For by grace you have been saved through faith; and this is not your own doing, it is the gift of God.

Ephesians 2:8 RSV

I, even I, am he who blots out your transgressions, for my own sake, and remembers your sins no more.

Isaiah 43:25

Let us draw near with a true heart in full assurance of faith, having our hearts sprinkled from an evil conscience and our bodies washed with pure water.

Hebrews 10:22 NKJV

Absolutely!

At age thirty-three, golfer Paul Azinger was at the top of his game. He had only one problem: a nagging pain in his right shoulder. After seeing the doctor, Paul received a call that changed his life. His doctor wanted him back in Los Angeles immediately for a biopsy. Paul forged a compromise: he'd do it as soon as he had played in the PGA Championship Tournament and the Ryder's Cup Challenge. He tried to convince himself he had tendonitis, but the pain grew worse. He had cancer.

13

Paul began chemotherapy. One morning while praying in his bedroom, he was wondering what would happen if he didn't get better. Suddenly the sun seemed to force its way through the blinds, and a powerful feeling of peace swelled within him. He knew with absolute assurance that God was with him.

Two years later, Paul rejoined the pro tour, his cancer gone. He says that his main goal in life now has shifted from winning to helping people see that "God is there for them."

Teach your children that God is always with them. Instruct them that even when their circumstances seem bleak, if they will trust in Him, He will take care of them.

Assurance

"All that the Father giveth me shall come to me; and him that cometh to me I will in no wise cast out."

John 6:37 KJV

14

I am sure that God who began the good work within you will keep right on helping you grow in his grace until his task within you is finally finished.

Philippians 1:6 TLB

"My sheep hear my voice, and I know them, and they follow me: And I give unto them eternal life; and they shall never perish, neither shall any man pluck them out of my hand."

John 10:27-28 KJV

If you confess with your mouth, "Jesus is Lord," and believe in your heart that God raised him from the dead, you will be saved.

Romans 10:9

Yes, Even These

Matthew was a tax collector—a hated man among the Jews for helping Rome tighten its occupation. Even so, Jesus loved Matthew and eventually chose him as one of His disciples.

Peter had a quick temper, his emotions easily triggered by circumstances. During the most critical hours of Jesus' life on earth, he denied knowing Jesus three times. Even so, Jesus loved Peter and empowered him to lead the early church.

Saul wreaked havoc on the church in Jerusalem, leading raids on the homes of Christians and imprisoning the devout. He consented to the death of Stephen and was one of the official witnesses of his execution. He even requested letters of authority to extend the persecution of the church to other cities, including Damascus. Even so, Jesus loved Saul, appeared to him in a light from heaven, and called him to repentance.

It is important for your children to learn that Jesus loves all people—regardless of their sins or character flaws. He loved all of us so much that he died on the Cross on our behalf. Your children must realize that He died, not just for them, but also for their enemies and for every person who has ever left them disappointed or frustrated.

Burdens

Do not be anxious about anything, but in everything, by prayer and petition, with thanksgiving, present your requests to God. And the peace of God, which transcends all understanding, will guard your hearts and your minds in Christ Jesus.

Philippians 4:6-7

16

The LORD preserveth the simple: I was brought low, and he helped me. Return unto thy rest, O my soul; for the LORD hath dealt bountifully with thee. For thou hast delivered my soul from death, mine eyes from tears, and my feet from falling.

Psalm 116:6-8 KJV

For I, the LORD your God, hold your right hand; it is I who say to you, "Fear not, I will help you."

Isaiah 41:13 RSV

"These things I have spoken unto you, that in me ye might have peace. In the world ye shall have tribulation: but be of good cheer; I have overcome the world."

John 16:33 KJV

Good from A to Z

Rachel and Jim owned a commercial building, half of which Jim used for his dental practice. For fifteen years, they had encountered no difficulty in renting out the other half. Then they lost their renter. They usually counted on this extra income to help pay their bills, so they began to worry when a real estate agent told them, "Forget about advertising for a while. Absolutely no one is renting."

To ease her financial stress, Rachel started swimming laps at her local YMCA pool. One day when she was feeling especially anxious, she decided to pray as she swam, using the alphabet to keep track of the number of laps. She focused on adjectives that described God, starting with the letter A. By the time she had completed twenty-six laps, an hour had passed, and her fears were gone. She knew God would provide.

A short time later, a physical therapist called to say she had seen the "For Rent" sign in the window, and she asked to see the office. It was exactly what she wanted, so she and her partner rented the space.

Explain to your children that when they take their eyes off of their problems and focus on God and His incredible attributes, their worries will fade away. Remind them that God's goodness stretches from A to Z!

Burdens

Cast thy burden upon the LORD, and he
shall sustain thee.

Psalm 55:22 KJV

18

"Come to me, all you who are weary and
burdened, and I will give you rest. Take my yoke
upon you and learn from me, for I am gentle and
humble in heart, and you will find rest for your
souls. For my yoke is easy and my burden is light."

Matthew 11:28-30

Humble yourselves, therefore, under God's mighty
hand, that he may lift you up in due time. Cast all
your anxiety on him because he cares for you.

I Peter 5:6-7

Carry each other's burdens, and in this way you
will fulfill the law of Christ.

Galatians 6:2

The Worry Table

A military chaplain once drew up a "Worry Table" based upon the problems men and women had brought to him through his years of service. He found their worries fit into the following categories:

- Worries about things that never happened— 40 percent
- Worries about past, unchangeable decisions—30 percent
- Worries about illness that never happened— 12 percent
- Worries about adults, children, and friends (who were able to take care of themselves)—10 percent
- Worries about real problems—8 percent

According to his chart, 92 percent of all our worries are about things we can't control—things which are better left to God. The truth is, anxiety is rooted in a failure to trust God.

Our worries show that we simply don't believe He is big enough or that He cares enough to help with our problems, give us the desires of our hearts, and keep us—and our loved ones—from harm.

Once your children know God's character, they will easily see that they worry for nothing most of the time. Remind them that God is more than big enough and cares more than enough to help them, bless them, and protect them. Teach them to give their worries to Him, and He will replace those worries with His peace.

Children

The promise is for you and your children and for all who are far off—for all whom the Lord our God will call.

Acts 2:39

20

When Jesus saw what was happening he was very much displeased with his disciples and said to them, "Let the children come to me, for the Kingdom of God belongs to such as they. Don't send them away!"

Mark 10:14 TLB

Children are a gift from God; they are his reward. Children born to a young man are like sharp arrows to defend him. Happy is the man who has his quiver full of them. That man shall have the help he needs when arguing with his enemies.

Psalm 127:3-5 TLB

Only take heed to yourself, and diligently keep yourself, lest you forget the things your eyes have seen, and lest they depart from your heart all the days of your life. And teach them to your children and your grandchildren.

Deuteronomy 4:9 NKJV

The Wind beneath Their Wings

When John was just a boy, he journeyed with his family across the American continent. It took the family a full year to make their way from coast to coast. As each sunset and sunrise glorified the sky, the Scottish father would take his children out to show them the sky and speak to them about how the cloud formations were surely "the robes of God."

Who can fathom the full impact this had on young John or how deeply rooted his reverence for nature became on this year-long journey? What we do know is that John Muir became one of America's greatest naturalists. His love for nature led him to the majestic mountains, the glacial meadows, and eventually to the icebound bays of Alaska. The lovely Muir Woods in northern California are named in his honor.

What are you "showing" your children today? What "wind" are you putting under their wings? What examples, what encouragement, what insights are you giving your child?

As the song declared so poignantly more than two decades ago: "You are the wind beneath my wings"—so is a parent's influence for each child.

Children

Train a child in the way he should go, and when he is old he will not turn from it.

Proverbs 22:6

22

He who spares the rod hates his son, but he who loves him is diligent to discipline him.

Proverbs 13:24 RSV

Discipline your son, for in that there is hope; do not be a willing party to his death.

Proverbs 19:18

The father of a righteous man has great joy; he who has a wise son delights in him.

Proverbs 23:24-25

Just Five More Minutes

A man sat on a park bench next to a woman looking out at the playground.

"That's my daughter," she said, pointing to a little girl who was gliding down the slide. Then, looking at her watch, she called to her daughter, "What do you say we go, Samantha?"

Samantha pleaded, "Just five minutes more, Mom. Please? Just five more minutes." The woman nodded, so the child continued to play to her heart's content.

Minutes later the mother stood and called, "Time to go now."

Again the girl pleaded, "Five more minutes, Mom, just five more minutes."

Her mother smiled and said, "Okay."

"My, you certainly are a patient mother," the man responded.

"Last year," the woman said, "our son Tommy was killed by a drunk driver while riding his bike near here. I never spent much time with Tommy, and now I'd give anything for just five more minutes with him. I vowed I wouldn't make the same mistake with Samantha. She thinks *she* has five more minutes to swing. Truth is, I get five more minutes with her."

There will be plenty of opportunity for your child to experience disappointment in life without you being the cause of it. Next time you become impatient with your child, ask yourself: *Would I really be in such a rush if this were my child's last day on earth?*

Comfort

Trust in him at all times, O people; pour out your hearts to him, for God is our refuge.

Psalm 62:8

24

You have turned for me my mourning into dancing; You have put off my sackcloth and clothed me with gladness.

Psalm 30:11 NKJV

[Jesus said]: "Therefore you too now have sorrow; but I will see you again, and your heart will rejoice, and no one [will] take your joy away from you."

John 16:22 NASB

When times are good, be happy; but when times are bad, consider: God has made the one as well as the other.

Ecclesiastes 7:14

Comforting Retreat

Have you ever explored a tidal pool? Low tide is the perfect time to find a myriad of creatures that have temporarily washed ashore from the depths of the sea.

People are often amazed that they can pick up these shelled creatures and stare at them eyeball to eyeball. The creatures rarely exhibit any form of overt fear, such as moving to attack or attempting to scurry away. The creatures simply withdraw into their shells, instinctively knowing they are safe as long as they remain in their strong, cozy shelters.

Likewise, we are safe when we remain in Christ. We are protected from the hassles of life and the fear of unknowns. Those things will come against us, much like the fingers of a brave and curious child trying to invade the sea creature's shell, but they have no power to harm us when we retreat into the shelter of Christ.

The Lord commanded us to learn to *abide* in Him and to *remain* steadfast in our faith. He tells us to *trust* in Him absolutely and to *shelter* ourselves under His strong wings and in the cleft of His rock-like presence. He delights when we *retreat* into His arms for comfort and tender expressions of love.

Rest in the Lord and trust in Him to give you wisdom as you raise your children. In doing so, you will not only receive the comfort you need, but you will also be teaching your children a valuable lesson about resting in the Lord.

Comfort

Many are the sorrows of the wicked; But he who trusts in the LORD, lovingkindness shall surround him.

Psalm 32:10 NASB

26

"Blessed are you who hunger now, for you will be satisfied. Blessed are you who weep now, for you will laugh."

Luke 6:21

The eyes of the LORD are on those who fear him, on those whose hope is in his unfailing love.

Psalm 33:18

You are my hiding place; You shall preserve me from trouble; You shall surround me with songs of deliverance.

Psalm 32:7 NKJV

Pa's Watch

One evening in Albany, New York, a man asked a sailor what time it was. The serviceman pulled out a huge watch and replied, "It's 7:20."

The man knew it was later, so he asked, "Your watch has stopped, hasn't it?"

"No," said the sailor, "I'm still on Mountain Standard Time. I'm from southern Utah. When I joined the navy, Pa gave me this watch. He said it'd help me remember home. When my watch says 5 A.M., I know Dad is rollin' out to milk the cows. And any night when it says 7:30, I know the whole family's around a well-spread table, and Dad's thankin' God for what's on it and askin' Him to watch over me. I can almost smell the hot biscuits and bacon.

"It's thinkin' about those things that makes me want to fight when the goin' gets tough," he concluded. "I can find out what time it is where I am, easy enough. What I want to know is, what time it is in Utah."

This serviceman's father had obviously set good examples for his son and had raised him to appreciate home and family values. He had acquired such strong faith that he was willing to fight for his country to preserve it.

Set good examples for your children. Raise them in a home that teaches strong values. This will not only be a great source of comfort for them, but it will also help to develop their character and strengthen their faith.[2]

Conflict

How good and pleasant it is when brothers live together in unity!

Psalm 133:1

28 It's harder to make amends with an offended friend than to capture a fortified city. Arguments separate friends like a gate locked with iron bars.

Proverbs 18:19 NLT

He will lead children and parents to love each other more, so that when I come, I won't bring doom to the land.

Malachi 4:6 CEV

"Therefore if you are presenting your offering at the altar, and there remember that your brother has something against you, leave your offering there before the altar, and go; first be reconciled to your brother, and then come and present your offering."

Matthew 5:23-24 NASB

Never Too Late

Stewart decided to visit his twenty-year-old son at college. He asked the young man what it had been like growing up with him as a father. "Well, Dad," he said, "I don't want to hurt your feelings, but you were never there."

"What do you mean?" Stewart asked. "I was home every evening. I never went anywhere!"

His son said, "I know, Dad, but if you were ever sad, I never knew it. You never seemed happy. I didn't know who you were. Most of the time," his voice began to crack, "I felt like I didn't have a father."

29

Stewart broke down and sobbed uncontrollably. "Can you believe it?" he said through his tears. "I was there, right in front of you, all that time, and yet you felt I was invisible."

He and his son decided to change things. They joined an outdoor club together, and on a deep-sea fishing trip he told his son, "I'm so angry at myself—and what I really regret is that I've hurt you so much—not by doing something mean, but because I failed to let you get to know me."

"Dad, I forgive you."

It's never too late to become a parent to your child! Don't let the fear of facing conflict keep you from reaping the benefits of relationship.

Conflict

Live in harmony with one another; be sympathetic,
love as brothers, be compassionate and humble.
Do not repay evil with evil or insult with insult,
but with blessing.

1 Peter 3:8-9

30

May the God of steadfastness and encouragement
grant you to live in such harmony with one
another, in accord with Christ Jesus, that together
you may with one voice glorify the God and
Father of our Lord Jesus Christ.

Romans 15:5-6 RSV

Try always to be led along together by the Holy
Spirit, and so be at peace with one another.

Ephesians 4:3 TLB

Don't grumble about each other, brothers. Are
you yourselves above criticism? For see! The great
Judge is coming.

James 5:9 TLB

The Tondelayo

In *The Fall of Fortresses,* Elmer Bendiner tells of a miracle that happened to him and a few others aboard their B-17 bomber, the *Tondelayo.* During a run over Kassel, Germany, the plane was barraged by Nazi antiaircraft guns. That in itself was not unusual, but on this particular flight the fuel tanks of the plane were hit. The following morning, the pilot Bohn Fawkes asked the crew chief for the shell as a souvenir of their unbelievable luck.

Bohn was then told that not just one shell had been found in the gas tanks, but eleven!

The shells were sent to the armorers to be defused. Later they informed the *Tondelayo* crew that when they opened the shells, they found no explosive charge in any of them. One of the shells, however, contained a carefully rolled piece of paper. On it was scrawled in the Czech language: "This is all we can do for you now." The miracle had not been one of misfired shells, but of peace-loving hearts.

If we want peace in our lives, we must disarm our weapons—our painful words, prideful looks, and hurtful attitudes. Teach your children to diffuse conflict in favor of unity, and God will flood their lives with His peace and love.

Confusion

Trust the Lord completely; don't ever trust yourself. In everything you do, put God first, and he will direct you and crown your efforts with success.

Proverbs 3:5-6 TLB

32

I will instruct thee and teach thee in the way which thou shalt go: I will guide thee with mine eye.

Psalm 32:8 KJV

Where envy and self-seeking exist, confusion and every evil thing are there.

James 3:16 NKJV

Your ears will hear a word behind you, "This is the way, walk in it," whenever you turn to the right or to the left.

Isaiah 30:21 NASB

Following the Guide

Many years ago when Egyptian troops conquered the region of Nubia, a regiment of soldiers crossed the desert with an Arab guide. Their water rations were limited, and the soldiers were suffering from great thirst. Suddenly, a beautiful lake appeared on the horizon. The soldiers insisted that their guide take them to its banks. The guide knew the desert well and recognized that what they were seeing was just a mirage. He told the soldiers that the lake was not real and refused to lose precious time by wandering from the designated course.

Angry words followed. The soldiers decided they didn't need the guide's advice and parted company from him. Yet as the soldiers moved toward the lake, it receded into the distance. Finally, they recognized that the lake was only burning sand. Raging thirst and horrible despair engulfed them. Without their guide, they were lost and without water. Not one of them survived.

Teach your children to be sure that what they seek today is not only within the realm of reality, but even more importantly, that it is part of God's plan for their lives. Any other goal is likely to be unworthy of their pursuits and may even be deadly.

Courage

Don't be afraid, for I am with you. Do not be
dismayed, for I am your God. I will strengthen
you. I will help you. I will uphold you with my
victorious right hand.

Isaiah 41:10 NLT

Be strong, and let your heart take courage,
All you who hope in the LORD.

Psalm 31:24 NASB

Be on your guard; stand firm in the faith;
be men of courage; be strong.

1 Corinthians 16:13

The fear of man brings a snare, But whoever
trusts in the LORD shall be safe.

Proverbs 29:25 NKJV

A Historic Resolution

Most people know of the Great Depression that occurred during the 1930s, but few know about the financial depression in the first half of the 1800s. Governments went into financial panic. Pennsylvania, one of the wealthier states at the time, rejected its debts—in effect declaring itself bankrupt. Illinois felt that with such a move made by its wealthy neighbor, it might be justified in doing likewise.

When Stephen Douglas heard of the proposal for bankruptcy, he strongly opposed it. Although ill at the time, he insisted that he be carried to the state legislature on a stretcher. Lying on his back, he made this historic resolution: "That Illinois be honest." The motion touched the hearts of every member of the state house, and the resolution was adopted with eagerness. The action by Illinois kept the practice of repudiation from spreading among the states. Many historians credit this move as a key reason why Illinois is one of the most prosperous states today.

Choosing the right direction sometimes means choosing the unpopular direction with the greatest amount of discomfort. Teach your children that there is no substitute for the rewards that can come at the end of such a journey.[3]

Courage

That he would grant unto us, that we being
delivered out of the hand of our enemies
might serve him without fear.

Luke 1:74 KJV

Be strong and courageous. Do not be afraid or
terrified for the LORD your God goes with
you; he will never leave you nor forsake you.

Deuteronomy 31:6

Christ gives me the strength to face anything.

Philippians 4:13 CEV

We say with confidence, "The Lord is my helper;
I will not be afraid. What can man do to me?"

Hebrews 13:6

The Courage to Risk

- To laugh is to risk appearing the fool.
- To weep is to risk appearing sentimental.
- To reach out to another is to risk involvement.
- To expose your feelings is to risk revealing your inner self.
- To place your dreams before the crowd is to risk loss.
- To love is to risk not being loved in return.
- To hope is to risk despair.
- To try is to risk failure.
- To live is to risk dying.
- Not to risk is the greatest risk of all.

"The paradox of courage," G.K. Chesterton once wrote, "is that a person must be a little careless of life in order to survive." Teach your children the difference between careless risk and the kind of risk that produces greatness.

Death or Loss

We know that in everything God works for good
with those who love him, who are called according
to his purpose.

Romans 8:28 RSV

38

I am convinced that nothing can ever separate us
from his love. Death can't, and life can't. The
angels can't, and the demons can't. Our fears for
today, our worries about tomorrow, and even the
powers of hell can't keep God's love away. Whether
we are high above the sky or in the deepest ocean,
nothing in all creation will ever be able to separate
us from the love of God that is revealed in Christ
Jesus our Lord.

Romans 8:38-39 NLT

If we live, we live to the Lord; and if we die,
we die to the Lord. So, whether we live or die,
we belong to the Lord.

Romans 14:8

The bodies we now have are weak and can die. But
they will be changed into bodies that are eternal.
Then the Scriptures will come true, "Death has lost
the battle! Where is its victory? Where is its sting?"

1 Corinthians 15:54-55 CEV

Every Exit Is an Entrance

Author-pastor John Claypool offers a reassuring perspective on the experience of loss:

> I've learned something through all my experiences—that every exit is also an entrance. Every time you walk out of something, you walk into something. I got into this world by dying in the womb—and it must have been painful to get ripped out of that familiar place—but that was the prerequisite of my getting into time and space. At the end of my life in history there's going to be a similar kind of transition experience. If we can get at the terror of death by saying it is a transformer rather than an annihilator, then perhaps we can get rid of the idea that death is a thief and is taking something that is rightfully ours, which is the basis of all the rage that I know.

Death is the ultimate experience of loss, of course, and it often overshadows all our other losses. Watching children grow up and out of our control can cause a painful sense of loss. May we all come to view our losses as "transformers rather than annihilators."

Death or Loss

To all who mourn in Israel, he will give beauty for ashes, joy instead of mourning, praise instead of despair.

Isaiah 61:3 NLT

40

"Blessed are those who mourn, for they will be comforted."

Matthew 5:4

For as the sufferings of Christ abound in us, so our consolation also abounds through Christ.

2 Corinthians 1:5 NKJV

Laugh with your happy friends when they're happy; share tears when they're down.

Romans 12:15 THE MESSAGE

Choosing Life

"Life is a test," Marnita Lloyd told her fellow classmates and teachers during graduation exercises at Detroit's Denby Technical and Preparatory High School. "You either pass or fail—it's up to you."

Marnita went on to a full scholarship at Wayne State University, but the road to academic achievement for this valedictorian was marked by plenty of setbacks and obstacles. When she was eleven, her brother was killed in a drug dispute. When she was sixteen, her mother died of heart disease. During her senior year, a sixteen-year-old friend was fatally stabbed at his locker and an eighteen-year-old friend was gunned down at a church carnival.

Marnita went to class rather than get involved in the commotion of the school slaying. She chose to stay home and study rather than participate in a neighborhood antiviolence parade after the carnival murder. "Those [parades] are good," she said, "but it won't help me study for my government test." Marnita kept her eyes on her personal goal: a medical career as an obstetrician-gynecologist. She chose to place her emphasis on new life rather than death.

Teach your children that death and loss are a natural part of life.[4]

Deliverance

Because he cleaves to me in love, I will deliver him; I will protect him, because he knows my name. When he calls to me, I will answer him; I will be with him in trouble, I will rescue him and honor him.

Psalm 91:14-15 RSV

42

He has rescued us out of the darkness and gloom of Satan's kingdom and brought us into the Kingdom of his dear Son.

Colossians 1:13 TLB

The Lord knoweth how to deliver the godly out of temptations, and to reserve the unjust unto the day of judgment to be punished.

2 Peter 2:9 KJV

Deliverance belongs to the LORD; thy blessing be upon thy people!

Psalm 3:8 RSV

Our Refuge and Strength

Norma Zimmer, a well-known singer for Lawrence Welk, had a difficult childhood. As a high school senior, she was invited to be a featured soloist at the University Christian Church in Seattle. When her parents heard she was going to sing a particular song, they both insisted on attending the service. She says about that morning, "I stole glances at the congregation, trying to find my parents . . . then in horror I saw them— weaving down the aisle in a state of disheveled intoxication. . . . I don't know how I ever got through that morning."

After she sang and took her seat, her cheeks burning from embarrassment, the pastor preached: "God is our refuge and strength, a tested help in time of trouble." She says, "I realized how desperate life in our family was without God, and that day I recommitted my life to Him . . . Jesus came into my life not only as Savior but for daily strength and direction."

God's deliverance is not only for the future, but for the present. He is a constant Help in times of trouble. If you daily rely on Him for deliverance and direction, you will not only receive the peace you need, but also you will be setting a tremendous example for your children!

Deliverance

When the righteous cry for help, the LORD hears,
and delivers them out of all their troubles.

Psalm 34:17 RSV

44

He who trusts in his own heart is a fool, But
whoever walks wisely will be delivered.

Proverbs 28:26 NKJV

The LORD is my rock, my fortress and my deliverer.

2 Samuel 22:2

But I am poor and needy; Yet the LORD thinks
upon me. You are my help and my deliverer;
Do not delay, O my God.

Psalm 40:17 NKJV

The Thundering Legion

The Militine Legion was one of the two most famous legions in the Roman army. It was also known as the "Thundering Legion." The nickname was given by the philosopher-emperor Marcus Aurelius in 176 A.D., during a military campaign against the Germans.

In their march northward, the Romans were encircled by precipitous mountains which were occupied by their enemies. In addition, due to a drought, they were tormented by great thirst. Then a member of the Praetorian Guard informed the emperor that the Militine Legion was made up of Christians who believed in the power of prayer. Although he himself had been a great persecutor of the Church, the emperor said, "Let them pray then." The soldiers bowed on the ground and earnestly sought God to deliver them in the name of Jesus Christ.

They had scarcely risen from their knees when a great thunderstorm arose. The storm drove their enemies from their strongholds and into their arms, where they pleaded for mercy. The storm also provided water to drink and ended the drought. The emperor renamed them the "Thundering Legion" and subsequently abated some of his persecution of the Christians in Rome.

Teach your children that prayer should be their first resort, instead of their last. Prayer and deliverance go hand in hand!

Discipline

Do not withhold discipline from a child; if you punish him with the rod, he will not die.

Proverbs 23:13

46

No discipline seems pleasant at the time, but painful. Later on, however, it produces a harvest of righteousness and peace for those who have been trained by it.

Hebrews 12:11

My son, do not make light of the Lord's discipline, and do not lose heart when he rebukes you, because the Lord disciplines those he loves, and he punishes everyone he accepts as a son.

Hebrews 12:5-6

Folly is bound up in the heart of a child, but the rod of discipline will drive it far from him.

Proverbs 22:15

A Non-Squawking Flight

On a recent flight, two small children who were not happy about being on an airplane disrupted everyone else's peace. Their cries and complaints filled the cabin as they climbed all over the seats and ran up and down the aisle. The parents did everything they could to calm the children down, but nothing worked. Finally, they just gave up and let the children run wild. It was obvious from the behavior of the little boy and his sister that they were not used to being disciplined.

Just before takeoff, a flight attendant stopped next to them and said with a big smile, "What is all this squawking up here?" After charming the fussy three-year-old and his older sister for a few minutes, the flight attendant bent down and whispered seriously, "I must remind you that this is a non-squawking flight."

The little ones became unbelievably quiet and remained that way during the entire flight, much to the relief of the rest of the passengers.

Your children's behavior affects everyone around them. Teach them to respect others by making every day a non-squawking journey.

Discipline

He who spares the rod hates his son, but he who loves him is careful to discipline him.

Proverbs 13:24

48

Our fathers disciplined us for a little while as they thought best; but God disciplines us for our good, that we may share in his holiness.

Hebrews 12:10

Discipline your son, for in that there is hope.

Proverbs 19:18

Endure hardship as discipline; God is treating you as sons. For what son is not disciplined by his father?

Hebrews 12:7

Too Late

In a Los Angeles park, Roy B. Zuck saw a large tree that had grown somewhat crooked. The oddest thing about the tree was that someone had placed an upright pole near it and tied it to the tree with ropes. But the tree had grown out so far from the place where the trunk came out of the ground that there was a lot of distance between the pole and the tree. It was too late for this pole to help the tree.

This often happens in the raising of children when parents allow them to run wild for the first fifteen years of their lives. When the parents realize their mistakes and try to correct or straighten out their children, sometimes they find that it's too late without intervention from an outside source.

Children require regular and consistent discipline. It creates limits and shows children that someone cares enough about them to set them on the right path. It is also a part of a loving relationship with your children and is necessary in helping them become responsible adults.[5]

Discontentment

All the days of the afflicted are evil, But he who is of a merry heart has a continual feast.

Proverbs 15:15 NKJV

50

Let not thine heart envy sinners: but be thou in the fear of the LORD all the day long. For surely there is an end; and thine expectation shall not be cut off.

Proverbs 23:17-18 KJV

Now godliness with contentment is great gain.

1 Timothy 6:6 NKJV

He who dwells in the shelter of the Most High will rest in the shadow of the Almighty.

Psalm 91:1

Contentment Is . . .

In her book, *Startled by Silence,* Ruth Senter tells the following story of what contentment means:

"I heard the voice, but I couldn't see the person.

"'Delores, I really appreciated the book you picked up for me. . . . I haven't been able to put the book down.'

"For a moment, the melodious voice was silent, then I heard it again.

"'Have you ever seen such a gorgeous day?'

"The voice was too good to be true. Who can be thankful at this time of morning? Probably some rich woman who has nothing to do all day but sip tea and read.

"I rounded the corner and came face to face with the youthful voice. Her yellow housekeeping uniform hung crisp and neat on her fiftyish frame—she was an employee of the facility at which I swam.

"I still had the yellow uniform on my mind as I sank down into the whirlpool. My two companions were deep in conversation.

"'The water is too hot, the whirlpool jets aren't strong enough . . . ' With a diamond-studded hand, one of them wiped the white suds out of his face.

"The yellow uniform and the diamond-studded ring stood out in striking, silent contrast, proof to me again that when God says, 'Godliness with contentment is great gain,' He really means it."

Discontentment

Let your conversation be without covetousness; and be content with such things as ye have: for he hath said, I will never leave thee, nor forsake thee.

Hebrews 13:5 KJV

52

I have learned in whatever state I am, to be content: I know how to be abased, and I know how to abound. Everywhere and in all things I have learned both to be full and to be hungry, both to abound and to suffer need. I can do all things through Christ who strengthens me.

Philippians 4:11-13 NKJV

We know that all things work together for good to them that love God, to them who are the called according to his purpose.

Romans 8:28 KJV

Not that we are sufficient of ourselves to think any thing as of ourselves; but our sufficiency is of God.

2 Corinthians 3:5 KJV

Contented Regardless

For decades, Grandpa had been stubborn and crabby. His wife, children, and grandchildren seemed unable to do anything that pleased him. As far as he was concerned, life was filled with nothing but bad times and big troubles. Eventually, his family expected nothing but a gruff growl from him.

Then overnight, Grandpa changed. Gentleness and optimism marked his new personality. Positive words and compliments poured from his lips, and he could even be heard giving joyful praise to the Lord. One of the family members noted, "I think maybe Grandpa found religion."

Another replied, "Maybe so, but maybe it's something else. I'm going to ask him what has happened." The young man went to his grandfather and said, "Gramps, what has caused you to change so suddenly?"

"Well, son," the old man replied, "I've been striving in the face of incredible problems all my life—and for what? The hope of a contented mind. It's done no good, nope, not one bit, so . . . I've decided to be content without it."

Remind your children never to start counting their troubles until they've counted at least a hundred of their blessings. By that time, they will have long forgotten what their troubles even were!

Discouragement

My mouth would encourage you; comfort
from my lips would bring you relief.
Job 16:5

54

You are my hiding place from every storm of life;
you even keep me from getting into trouble!
You surround me with songs of victory.
Psalm 32:7 TLB

Those who know you, LORD, will trust you; you
do not abandon anyone who comes to you.
Psalm 9:10 TEV

When life is good, enjoy it. But when life is hard,
remember: God gives good times and hard times.
Ecclesiastes 7:14 NCV

You Mustn't Quit

When things go wrong, as they sometimes will,
When the road you're trudging seems
    all uphill,
When the funds are low and the debts are high
And you want to smile, but you have to sigh,
When care is pressing you down a bit,
Rest! If you must—but never quit.
Life is queer, with its twists and turns,
As every one of us sometimes learns,
And many a failure turns about
When he might have won if he'd stuck it out;
Stick to your task, though the pace seems slow —
You may succeed with one more blow.
Success is failure turned inside out —
The silver tint of the clouds of doubt —
And you never can tell how close you are,
It may be near when it seems afar;
So stick to the fight when you're hardest hit —
It's when things seem worst that
YOU MUSTN'T QUIT.

—Unknown

Discouragement

We gladly suffer, because we know that suffering helps us to endure. And endurance builds character, which gives us a hope that will never disappoint us. All of this happens because God has given us the Holy Spirit, who fills our hearts with his love.

Romans 5:3-5 CEV

56

[Love] always protects, always trusts, always hopes, always perseveres.

1 Corinthians 13:7

Blessed is the man who endures trial, for when he has stood the test he will receive the crown of life which God has promised to those who love him.

James 1:12 RSV

May the Lord direct your hearts into God's love and Christ's perseverance.

2 Thessalonians 3:5

God's Promise

A legal secretary was disgusted and depressed as she left work one rainy afternoon.

She had been hearing about other people's problems all day long, which wasn't new and usually didn't bother her, but this day had also been filled with injustice. A client came in crying because her estranged husband had taken their young children and wouldn't let her see them. Another client who had worked hard all his life and was now disabled had been denied Social Security disability benefits. His case would have to be appealed.

As she stepped out of the building, the rain added more gloom to her dreary outlook. She walked to her car still thinking about all the injustices of the world. As she drove through town, she silently pleaded with God to do something to cheer her up. Just then, she stopped at a red light. There in the sky beyond the traffic was a bright, exhilarating rainbow that brought tears of relief and joy to her eyes. God did care! The rainbow reminded her of God's compassion for His people and the promise that Jesus will return someday.

Teach your children to look for the rainbow when the injustices of life and other problems get them down![6]

Encouragement

God's love, though, is ever and always, eternally present to all who fear him, making everything right for them and their children as they follow his Covenant ways and remember to do whatever he said.

Psalm 103:17-18 THE MESSAGE

Trust in the Lord instead. Be kind and good to others; then you will live safely here in the land and prosper, feeding in safety. Be delighted with the Lord. Then he will give you all your heart's desires.

Psalm 37:3-4 TLB

The humble will see their God at work and be glad. Let all who seek God's help live in joy.

Psalm 69:32 NLT

Exhort one another daily, while it is called "Today," lest any of you be hardened through the deceitfulness of sin.

Hebrews 3:13 NKJV

58

True Riches

One day the Reverend John Newton called upon a Christian family who had suffered the loss of all they possessed in a devastating fire. He greeted the wife and mother of the family by saying, "I give you joy."

The woman seemed surprised at his words—almost offended—and replied, "What! Joy that all my property is consumed?"

"Oh, no," Newton answered, "but joy that you have so much property that fire cannot touch."

His words reminded her of the true riches of her life, those things that she valued beyond measure: her husband, whom she loved very much; her children, the light of her life; the good health that they all possessed; their joy in each other; their faith in God; the love of an extended family and friends; and their prayers for a future together.

None of these riches can be bought, bargained, or appraised. They come from within the heart and in the joy and peace of mind that comes from our belief in Jesus Christ. Surely it was His hand that brought her family safely through their ordeal.

What simple words of encouragement can you give to your children?[7]

Encouragement

The righteous face many troubles, but the LORD rescues them from each and every one.

Psalm 34:19 NLT

60

The Lord says, "If you love me and truly know who I am, I will rescue you and keep you safe. When you are in trouble, call out to me. I will answer and be there to protect and honor you."

Psalm 91:14-15 CEV

"These things I have spoken unto you, that in me ye might have peace. In the world ye shall have tribulation: but be of good cheer; I have overcome the world."

John 16:33 KJV

Humble yourselves therefore under the mighty hand of God, that in due time he may exalt you. Cast all your anxieties on him, for he cares about you.

1 Peter 5:6-7 RSV

The Right Path

Thomas Edison wrote the following tribute to his mother:

I did not have my mother long, but she cast over me a good influence that lasted all my life. The good effects of her early training I can never lose. If it had not been for her appreciation and her faith in me at a critical time in my experience, I would never likely have become an inventor. I was always a careless boy, and with a mother of different mental caliber, I would have turned out badly. But her firmness, her sweetness, her goodness were potent powers to keep me on the right path. My mother was the making of me. The memory of her will always be a blessing to me.

Parents, reassure your children that you discipline them for the things they do and not for the people they are. Tell them of your love for them, and show them how important they are in your eyes. Encourage, praise, and respect their efforts. Make a memory for your children that will be a blessing to them just as Thomas Edison's mother made for him.[8]

Failure

I am very happy to brag about my weaknesses.
Then Christ's power can live in me.

2 Corinthians 12:9 NCV

62

Our High Priest is not one who cannot feel
sympathy for our weaknesses. . . . Let us have
cofidence, then, and approach God's throne,
where there is grace. There we will receive mercy
and find grace to help us just when we need it.

Hebrews 4:15-16 TEV

If we believe not, yet he abideth faithful: he
cannot deny himself.

2 Timothy 2:13 KJV

Plans go wrong for lack of advice; many
counselors bring success.

Proverbs 15:22 NLT

Floating Soap

The best-selling products for Procter and Gamble in 1879 were candles. Then Thomas Edison invented the light bulb, and it looked as if candles might become obsolete, and the company would be in trouble. Their fears became reality when the market for candles plummeted. The economic forecast for the company seemed bleak.

However, about this time, a forgetful employee at a small factory in Cincinnati forgot to turn off his machine when he went to lunch. The result was a frothing mass of lather filled with air bubbles. He almost threw the mess away, but instead made it into soap. The soap floated, and thus Ivory soap was born. It became the mainstay of Procter and Gamble. Destiny had played a dramatic part in pulling the struggling company out of bankruptcy.

Why was floating soap so special? During that time, some people bathed in the river. Floating soap would never sink and, as a result, would not be lost. Ivory soap ultimately became a best-seller across the country.

Teach your children to use their energy and creativity to turn their mistakes into successes![9]

Failure

If God is for us, who can be against us? He who did not spare his own Son, but gave him up for us all—how will he not also, along with him, graciously give us all things?

Romans 8:31-32

64

Now thanks be to God who always leads us in triumph in Christ, and through us diffuses the fragrance of His knowledge in every place.

2 Corinthians 2:14 NKJV

All of us have sinned and fallen short of God's glory. But God treats us much better than we deserve, and because of Christ Jesus, he freely accepts us and sets us free from our sins.

Romans 3:23-24 CEV

God-loyal people don't stay down long; soon they're up on their feet, while the wicked end up flat on their faces.

Proverbs 24:16 THE MESSAGE

Giving God All

*J*anette Oke, a best-selling novelist with more than forty books to her credit, is considered the modern-day "pioneer author" for Christian fiction. When she first decided to write, she said to God, "Lord, I'm going to write this book. If it works, and if I discover I have talent, I'll give it all to You."

Janette sensed God was not pleased with the bargain she was trying to strike with Him. She felt in her heart as if He were responding, *If you're serious about this, then I want everything before you start.* Thus she gave Him her ambitions and dreams, and she trusted Him with the outcome of her efforts. She left it up to Him to teach her, whether she was successful or not. And a shelf of novels later, Janette Oke has proven "God can teach spiritual truths through fictional characters."

The greatest step of faith is to trust God *before* we see the results of our efforts. Whether we fail or succeed, God will still be with us. God doesn't ask for our best, He asks us for ourselves. Be sure your children know that when they give Him everything, He can use even their failures to bring them to eventual success.

Faith

What is faith? It is the confident assurance that
what we hope for is going to happen. It is the
evidence of things we cannot yet see.

Hebrews 11:1 NLT

Above all, taking the shield of faith, wherewith
ye shall be able to quench all the fiery darts
of the wicked.

Ephesians 6:16 KJV

We walk by faith, not by sight.

2 Corinthians 5:7 NKJV

"Everything is possible for him who believes."

Mark 9:23

The Red Sweater

John Croyle told the following story in *Focus on the Family* magazine:

One day a father took his children for a boat ride. They were traveling downriver when suddenly, the motor stopped. When the father looked behind him, he noticed a red sweater tangled up in the propeller. Then his young son yelled, "Sherry fell in!"

In horror the father saw his little girl entwined in the propeller of the boat. She was submerged just beneath the surface of the water, looking straight into the eyes of her father and holding her breath. He jumped into the water and tried to push the motor up, but the heavy engine wouldn't budge. Time was running out. Desperately, the father filled his own lungs with air and dipped below the surface. Then he took a knife and quickly cut the sweater from the propeller and lifted his daughter into the boat. She was rushed to the hospital.

When the crisis was over, the doctors and nurses asked the girl, "How come you didn't panic?"

"Well, we've grown up on the river," Sherry said, "and my dad always taught us that if you panic, you die. Besides, I knew my daddy would come and get me."

Children have such inherent trust in their parents. Teach your children to have this same simple faith toward God.[10]

Faith

When I look at the night sky and see the work of
your fingers—the moon and the stars you have set
in place—what are mortals that you should think
of us, mere humans that you should care for us?
For you made us only a little lower than God,
and you crowned us with glory and honor.

Psalm 8:3-5 NLT

Let love and faithfulness never leave you; bind
them around your neck, write them on the tablet
of your heart.

Proverbs 3:3

Every child of God can defeat the world, and
our faith is what gives us this victory.

1 John 5:4 CEV

"His master said to him, 'Well done, good and
faithful servant; you have been faithful over a
little, I will set you over much; enter into the joy
of your master.'"

Matthew 25:21 RSV

Nothing but Weeds

The great English poet Samuel Taylor Coleridge was once talking with a man who told him that he did not believe in giving children any religious training whatsoever. His philosophy was that children's minds should not be biased in any direction, but when they came to years of discretion, they should be permitted to choose their religious opinions for themselves. Mr. Coleridge said nothing, but after a while he asked his visitor if he would like to see his garden. The man replied that he would, and Coleridge took him out into the garden where only weeds were growing. The man looked at Coleridge in surprise and said, "Why, this is not a garden! There are nothing but weeds here!"

"Well, you see," answered Coleridge, "I did not wish to infringe upon the liberty of the garden in any way. I was just giving the garden a chance to express itself and to choose its own production."

Are you allowing your children to make all the decisions about their Christian education, or will you build a foundation in them on which to base their faith?[11]

Family

Choose for yourselves this day whom you will
serve. . . . But as for me and my house, we will
serve the LORD.

Joshua 24:15 NKJV

70

Be ye kind one to another, tender-hearted,
forgiving one another, even as God for Christ's
sake hath forgiven you.

Ephesians 4:32 KJV

Teach a child to choose the right path, and when
he is older he will remain upon it.

Proverbs 22:6 TLB

Children, obey your parents in the Lord, for this is
right. "Honor your father and mother"—which is
the first commandment with a promise—"that it
may go well with you and that you may enjoy long
life on the earth."

Ephesians 6:1–3

Clean Music Only

In an interview published in *People Weekly*, gospel singer CeCe Winans talked candidly about raising her children. She had grown up in a Christian home and was not even allowed to wear makeup until she was eighteen, so she wasn't about to embrace pop rock professionally or personally.

"I don't listen to secular music at home," said Winans, who lives in Nashville with her husband and manager, Alvin Love, and their kids, Alvin III and Ashley. "Very seldom do you find a mainstream artist who does only clean music. It's hard for me to wonder whether my children are going to listen to just the clean songs, so it's better to eliminate that music altogether."

CeCe made it clear that parents are responsible for the atmosphere that surrounds their children in the home. She understood her responsibilities and eliminated those things that she felt were detrimental to her children's spiritual growth.

Parents have many difficult decisions to make in the raising of their children. Often that means they have to give up something for themselves to substitute positive influences and reinforce the values of faith, hope, and love in the home.[12]

Family

He will direct his children and his household after him to keep the way of the LORD by doing what is right and just.

Genesis 18:19

72

Children, obey your parents in the Lord, for this is right. HONOR YOUR FATHER AND MOTHER (which is the first commandment with a promise), SO THAT IT MAY BE WELL WITH YOU, AND THAT YOU MAY LIVE LONG ON THE EARTH.

Ephesians 6:1-3 NASB

Be very careful never to forget what you have seen God doing for you. May his miracles have a deep and permanent effect upon your lives! Tell your children and your grandchildren about the glorious miracles he did.

Deuteronomy 4:9 TLB

But if anyone does not provide for his own, and especially for those of his household, he has denied the faith, and is worse than an unbeliever.

1 Timothy 5:8 NASB

Pete's Presents

During the Depression, many families could scarcely afford the bare essentials, much less Christmas presents. "But, I'll tell you what we can do," a father said to his six-year-old son, Pete. "We can use our imaginations and make pictures of the presents we would like to give each other."

For the next few days, each member of the family worked secretly, but joyfully. On Christmas morning huddled around a tree decorated with a few pitiful decorations, the family exchanged the presents they had created. Daddy got a shiny black limousine and a red motor boat. Mom received a diamond bracelet and a new hat. Little Pete had fun opening his gifts: a drawing of a swimming pool and pictures of toys cut from magazines.

Then it was Pete's turn to give his presents. With great delight, he handed his parents a brightly colored crayon drawing of three people—man, woman, and little boy. They had their arms around one another, and under the picture was one word: "US." Even though other Christmases were far more prosperous for this family, no Christmas in the family's memory stands out as more precious than the year they discovered their greatest gift was each other.

Teach your children the importance of family. Impress upon them the incredible value of loving relationships within the home.[13]

Favor

Never let loyalty and kindness get away from you!
Wear them like a necklace; write them deep within
your heart. Then you will find favor with both God
and people, and you will gain a good reputation.

Proverbs 3:3-4 NLT

Jesus grew in wisdom and stature, and in favor
with God and men.

Luke 2:52

But God was with him and delivered him out of all
his troubles, and gave him favor and wisdom in the
presence of Pharaoh, king of Egypt; and he made
him governor over Egypt and all his house.

Acts 7:9-10 NKJV

Fools don't care if they are wrong, but God is
pleased when people do right.

Proverbs 14:9 CEV

74

The Favor of God

The story is told of a king who owned a valuable diamond, one of the rarest and most perfect in the world. One day the diamond fell, and a deep scratch marred its face. The king summoned the best diamond experts in the land to correct the blemish, but they all agreed they could not remove the scratch without cutting away a good part of the surface, thus reducing the weight and value of the diamond.

Finally one expert appeared and assured him that he could fix the diamond without reducing its value. His confidence was convincing, and the king gave the diamond to the man. In a few days, the artisan returned the diamond to the king, who was amazed to find that the ugly scratch was gone, and in its place a beautiful rose was etched. The former scratch had become the stem of an exquisite flower!

Any mistake we make in life may temporarily mar our reputation. But impress upon your children that if they stick to what they know is right and continue to conform their will to God's, they can trust Him to turn the "scratches" on their souls into part of His signature—that's what it means to have God's favor.

Favor

For surely, O LORD, you bless the righteous; you surround them with your favor as with a shield.
Psalm 5:12

76

A good name is to be chosen rather than great riches, Loving favor rather than silver and gold.
Proverbs 22:1 NKJV

They did not conquer by their own strength and skill, but by your mighty power and because you smiled upon them and favored them.
Psalm 44:3 TLB

Whoever finds me finds life and wins approval from the LORD.
Proverbs 8:35 NLT

Favor for a Lifetime

The Psalms tell us that God's favor is for a lifetime. Wherever we go in life, whatever circumstances we face, God looks upon us with His favor and desires to show us His loving-kindness.

In *Unto the Hills,* Billy Graham reminds us of the story of God's favor toward Joseph. He writes:

> Joseph would never have been of use to God had he not been sold into slavery by brothers who hated him and wrongly accused by Potiphar, who put in him prison. Even after he had told Pharaoh's cupbearer he would be restored to the king's court and asked him to tell Pharaoh of his unjust imprisonment, Joseph had to wait two more years for release from prison.

All of this was God's preparation for Joseph's ultimate rise to a position of power and authority second only to that of Pharaoh himself, a position he used to feed all of Israel during a famine.

As we wait upon the Lord, God may sometimes seem slow in coming to help us, but He never comes too late. His timing is always perfect. How could it not be so from a God who favors us, as we do our children, for a lifetime?

Teach your children to trust God and to wait patiently for His perfect timing!

Fear

My flesh and my heart may fail, But God is the
strength of my heart and my portion forever.

Psalm 73:26 NASB

In the day of my trouble I will call upon You,
For You will answer me.

Psalm 86:7 NKJV

Let us be bold, then, and say, "The Lord is
my helper, I will not be afraid. What can anyone
do to me?"

Hebrews 13:6 TEV

God hath not given us the spirit of fear; but
of power, and of love, and of a sound mind.

2 Timothy 1:7 KJV

A Cleft in the Rock

A little boy and his big sister went out for a walk one day and decided to take a shortcut home by walking through a long, narrow railroad tunnel. For safety reasons, the railroad company had built small clefts next to the track in the tunnel so that if people got caught when a train was passing through, they might save themselves.

The little boy and girl had walked some distance into the tunnel when they heard a train coming. They were frightened at first, but the sister put her little brother in one cleft, and she hurried and hid in another. As the train came thundering toward them, the sister cried out, "Johnny, cling close to the rock!"

After the train had passed through the tunnel, the sister went to retrieve her brother. They both were safe.

When the train of life is barreling toward you in a dark tunnel—when your problems seem overwhelming—cling to the Rock. His name is Jesus Christ. Trust Him with your life, and teach your children to trust Him as well.[14]

Fear

GOD is our refuge and strength, A very present
help in trouble. Therefore we will not fear,
though the earth should change, And though
the mountains slip into the heart of the sea.

Psalm 46:1-2 NASB

80

My slanderers pursue me all day long; many are
attacking me in their pride. When I am afraid,
I will trust in you. In God, whose word I praise,
in God I trust; I will not be afraid. What can
mortal man do to me?

Psalm 56:2-4

That he would grant unto us, that we, being
delivered out of the hand of our enemies,
might serve him without fear.

Luke 1:74 KJV

Be glad for the chance to suffer as Christ suffered.
It will prepare you for even greater happiness when
he makes his glorious return. Count it a blessing
when you suffer for being a Christian. This shows
that God's glorious Spirit is with you.

1 Peter 4:13-14 CEV

Tigers in the Dark

One night at a circus that drew a packed audience of children and their parents, the tiger trainer came out to perform. After bowing to loud applause, he went into the cage. A hush drifted over the audience as the door was locked behind him.

Suddenly, as the trainer skillfully put the tigers through their paces, everyone heard a loud *Pop!* followed by the complete blackout of a power failure. For several long minutes the trainer was locked in the dark with the tigers, knowing they could see him with their powerful night vision, but he could not see them. A whip and a small kitchen chair seemed meager protection.

Finally the lights came back on, and the trainer finished his performance. Later, in a TV interview, he admitted his first chilling fears. Then he realized that the tigers did not know he could not see them. "I just cracked my whip and talked to them," he said, "until the lights came on."

At some point in life everyone will confront the terror of "tigers in the dark." Assure your children that with God's help, their fears will never be able to win a victory over them.

Finances

Two things I ask of you, O LORD; do not refuse me before I die: Keep falsehood and lies far from me; give me neither poverty nor riches, but give me only my daily bread. Otherwise, I may have too much and disown you and say, "Who is the LORD?" Or I may become poor and steal, and so dishonor the name of my God.

Proverbs 30:7-9

If you are thirsty, come and drink water! If you don't have any money, come, eat what you want! Drink wine and milk without paying a cent. Why waste your money on what really isn't food? Why work hard for something that doesn't satisfy? Listen carefully to me, and you will enjoy the very best foods.

Isaiah 55:1-2 CEV

He that loveth silver shall not be satisfied with silver; nor he that loveth abundance with increase: this is also vanity.

Ecclesiastes 5:10 KJV

"He will give you all you need from day to day if you live for him and make the Kingdom of God your primary concern."

Matthew 6:33 NLT

82

What Would Jesus Drive?

O n his sixteenth birthday, Danny and his father had an important heart-to-heart talk about cars. "When can I drive the family car?" Danny wanted to know.

"Son," his father began, "driving a car costs money and takes maturity. I want you to show me you're up to it. First, I want you to improve your grades. Second, I want you to read your Bible every day. And finally, I want you to get a haircut."

So Danny began the task of fulfilling his father's requirements. Next time grade reports came out, Danny came to his dad with a big smile, and said, "Look, Dad, all A's and B's. Now can I drive?"

"Great, son," his father said. You're one-third of the way there. Have you been reading the Bible daily?"

"Yes," Danny replied.

"Fine. You're two-thirds there. Now, when are you going to get that haircut?"

Danny frowned and said, "I don't see what a haircut has to do with driving. Jesus had long hair, right?"

"True," his dad replied. "And Jesus walked everywhere he went."

Getting through important passages in a child's life can bring tension and conflict, especially when money is involved. Strive, instead, to find humor in these situations, and choose to make them times of fun and increased closeness.

Finances

"When you give to someone, don't tell your left hand what your right hand is doing. Give your gifts in secret, and your Father, who knows all secrets, will reward you."

Matthew 6:3-4 NLT

84

"Do not store up for yourselves treasures on earth, where moth and rust destroy, and where thieves break in and steal. But store up for yourselves treasures in heaven, where moth and rust do not destroy, and where thieves do not break in and steal."

Matthew 6:19-20

"Therefore all things whatsoever ye would that men should do to you, do ye even so to them: for this is the law and the prophets."

Matthew 7:12 KJV

We brought nothing into the world, and we cannot take anything out of the world.

1 Timothy 6:7 RSV

Whoever Has the Gold
Makes the Rules

In Seoul, Korea, a wealthy visiting American textile executive was the after-dinner speaker for a large organization of Korean business leaders. To get his audience in a positive mood, the speaker told a rather long and rambling story that he thought was funny. Then he waited for the translator to relay it to his listeners.

After only a few words, the audience laughed uproariously and applauded at length. The speaker was so surprised he was barely able to complete his address. As soon as he was finished, he headed straight for the translator and complimented him for his efforts.

"I especially appreciate the way you translated my joke," he said. "I think it's wonderful that you helped me make such a good impression—and especially how you were able to shorten it in Korean."

"Think nothing of it," the interpreter replied. "I merely said, 'Man with big checkbook has told funny story. Do what you think is appropriate.'"

Our lore is packed with stories that illustrate, humorously or not, the fact that too often our society has inverted the Golden Rule to read: "Whoever has the gold makes the rules." What values do your children pick up when they observe your attitude toward money? Make sure that you are instilling the type of financial values that will equip them to live a Godly life.

Forgiveness

Let the wicked leave their way of life and change their way of thinking. Let them turn to the LORD, our God; he is merciful and quick to forgive.

Isaiah 55:7 TEV

86

"Come now, and let us reason together," Says the LORD, "Though your sins are as scarlet, They will be as white as snow; Though they are red like crimson, They will be like wool."

Isaiah 1:18 NASB

Blessed is he whose transgressions are forgiven, whose sins are covered.

Psalm 32:1

Be kind to each other, tenderhearted, forgiving one another, just as God has forgiven you because you belong to Christ.

Ephesians 4:32 TLB

No Fishing

The story is told of a boy and his mother who went to a shopping mall. The boy acted badly–demanding this and that, running away from his mother and hiding, whining that he wanted something to eat or drink, interrupting her while she was attempting to talk to sales clerks or make a purchase. In total exasperation, she finally gave up and returned to the car.

As they were driving home, the boy could sense her displeasure, and he said, "I learned last week in Sunday school that when we ask God to forgive us when we are bad, He does. Does he really do that?"

The mother replied, "Yes, He does."

The boy continued, "And the teacher said that when He forgives us, He throws ours sins into the deepest sea. Does he do that, Mom?"

The mother responded, "Yes, that's what the Bible says."

The boy was silent for a moment, and then he said, "I've asked God to forgive me for acting bad at the mall, but I bet when we get home, you're going to go fishing for those sins, aren't you?"

Children will err; that's a reality. Once you administer the appropriate discipline, throw the transgression in the sea and resist the urge to fish it up.

Forgiveness

If we confess our sins, he is faithful and just
to forgive us our sins, and to cleanse us from
all unrighteousness.

1 John 1:9 KJV

88

You, LORD, are good, and ready to forgive, And
abundant in mercy to all those who call upon You.

Psalm 86:5 NKJV

[The LORD says]: "I, I am the One who forgives
all your sins, for my sake; I will not remember
your sins."

Isaiah 43:25 NCV

If my people will humble themselves and pray,
and search for me, and turn from their wicked
ways, I will hear them from heaven and forgive
their sins and heal their land.

2 Chronicles 7:14 TLB

A White Handkerchief

Once upon a time there was a young man who left home, denouncing his father and mother. He wanted nothing to do with them again. Yet years later, he felt led to return home to see his parents. He wrote a letter to his mother, begging for her forgiveness. He asked that if she would let him come back home, to hang a white handkerchief on the clothesline in the backyard. The train passed near the rear of their house, and he said that if the handkerchief were there as he passed by, he would know that she would let him come home.

As he passed by on the train, to his amazement, there was not a white handkerchief on the line; however, a number of white sheets flapped in the breeze. How great was the love of that mother for her son! It was a small thing to hang sheets on the line, but what great love it conveyed!

A mother's heart is always big enough to hold the love she has for all her children and the forgiveness for the wrongs done and said by them. That capacity for forgiveness is a part of a mother's love and the love God has for us.[15]

Frustration

Call to Me, and I will answer you, and show you
great and mighty things, which you do not know.

Jeremiah 33:3 NKJV

90

We know that all things work together for good
to them that love God, to them who are the
called according to his purpose.

Romans 8:28 KJV

Encourage the exhausted, and strengthen the
feeble. Say to those with anxious heart, "Take
courage, fear not. Behold, your God will come."

Isaiah 35:3-4 NASB

God is faithful; he will not let you be tempted
beyond what you can bear. But when you are
tempted, he will also provide a way out so that
you can stand up under it.

1 Corinthians 10:13

Learning to Fly

There is an old legend that says God first created birds without wings. In due time, God made wings and said to the birds, "Come, take up these burdens and bear them."

The birds tried picking up the wings in their beaks, but they were too heavy. Next they tried picking them up with their claws, but they were too large. At last one of the birds managed to lift the wings onto its shoulders where it was possible to carry them.

Before long, the wings began to grow and soon had attached themselves to the birds' bodies. One of the birds began to flap its wings and soar in the air above! Soon others followed its example. What had been a heavy burden now became the instrument that enabled the birds to go where they could never go before.

As a parent, it's easy to feel as though you will never get through the next day, much less the next year. The sleepless nights of late feedings and colic, the endless days of the "terrible twos," homework, parent conferences, preadolescence, and teenagers—can seem like a huge burden. However, remember the legend of the birds and their wings, and know that God will be there for you.[16]

Frustration

The LORD says, "My thoughts are not like your thoughts. Your ways are not like my ways."

Isaiah 55:8 NCV

92

If God is on our side, who can ever be against us? Since he did not spare even his own Son for us but gave him up for us all, won't he also surely give us everything else?

Romans 8:31-32 TLB

Blessed is the man who perseveres under trial, because when he has stood the test, he will receive the crown of life that God has promised to those who love him.

James 1:12

Though I walk in the midst of trouble, You will revive me; You will stretch out Your hand Against the wrath of my enemies, And Your right hand will save me. The LORD will perfect that which concerns me.

Psalm 138:7-8 NKJV

Refusing to Quit

Sparky never had much going for him. He failed every subject in the eighth grade and several in high school. He was awkward, both physically and socially. Sparky was a teenager who never quite fit in anywhere. He did make the golf team, but then lost the most important match of the season. During his high school years, he never once asked a girl out on a date.

The most important thing in Sparky's life was his drawing. He was proud of his artwork, even though no one else appreciated it. He submitted cartoons to the editors of his high school yearbook, but they were rejected. He sent samples of his artwork to the Walt Disney Studios. Once again, his work was rejected.

Sparky refused to quit! He continued to have confidence in his ability to create art. After being turned down by Walt Disney, he decided to write his own autobiography in cartoons. The character he created was Charlie Brown, who became famous worldwide. Sparky was Charles Schulz, creator of the *Peanuts* comic strip. What a loss it would have been if Sparky had quit!

Teach your children never to give up on their dreams.[17]

God's Love

Now these three remain: faith, hope and love.
But the greatest of these is love.

1 Corinthians 13:13

94

Pursue a godly life, along with faith, love,
perseverance, and gentleness.

1 Timothy 6:11 NLT

Above all things have fervent love for one another,
for "love will cover a multitude of sins."

1 Peter 4:8 NKJV

Above all these put on love, which binds everything
together in perfect harmony.

Colossians 3:14 RSV

Jesus Loves Me

A minister received a call from a friend she had not seen in two years. The friend said, "My husband is leaving me for another woman. I need for you to pray with me."

The minister replied, "Come quickly."

When her friend arrived, the minister could not help but notice that she was carelessly dressed, had gained weight, and had failed to comb her hair or put on makeup. As they began to converse, the friend admitted to being an uninteresting, nagging wife and a sloppy housekeeper. The minister quickly concluded to herself, *My friend has grown to hate herself!*

When her friend paused to ask for her advice, the minister said only, "Will you join me in a song?" Surprised, her friend agreed. The minister began to sing, "Jesus loves me, this I know."

Her friend joined in, tears flooding her eyes. "If Jesus loves me, I must love myself, too," she concluded.

Amazing changes followed. Because she felt loved and lovable, this woman was transformed into the confident woman she once had been. In the process, she recaptured her husband's heart.

We can never accept God's love beyond the degree to which we are willing to love ourselves. Teach your children to see themselves the way God sees them. Then they will be able to fully grasp the amazing love of God and will want to pass it on to others.

God's Love

"For God so loved the world that he gave his only Son, that whoever believes in him should not perish but have eternal life."

John 3:16 RSV

He will love thee, and bless thee, and multiply thee.

Deuteronomy 7:13 KJV

The LORD sets prisoners free, the LORD gives sight to the blind, the LORD lifts up those who are bowed down, the LORD loves the righteous.

Psalm 146:7-8

The LORD your God is with you, he is mighty to save. He will take great delight in you, he will quiet you with his love, he will rejoice over you with singing.

Zephaniah 3:17

Adopted to Belong

A Sunday school superintendent was registering two new sisters in Sunday school. She asked their ages and birthdays, so she could place them in the appropriate classes. The bolder of the two replied, "We're both seven. My birthday is April 8, and my sister's birthday is April 20."

The superintendent replied, "But that's not possible, girls."

The quieter sister spoke up. "No, it's true. One of us is adopted."

"Oh?" asked the superintendent. "Which one?"

The two sisters looked at each other and smiled. The bolder one said, "We asked Dad that same question awhile ago, but he just looked at us and said he loved us both equally, and he couldn't remember anymore which one of us was adopted."

What a wonderful analogy of God's love! The Apostle Paul wrote to the Romans: "Now if we are [God's] children, then we are heirs—heirs of God and co-heirs with Christ" (Romans 8:17). In essence, as adopted sons and daughters of God, we fully share in the inheritance of His only begotten Son, Jesus. Our Heavenly Father has adopted us and loves us just as much as His beloved Son.

Be affectionate with your children and purpose to love them unconditionally. In doing this, you will be modeling for them the incredible, unfailing love of their Father God. Teach them to trust in His love and rest in His promises!

Guidance

Ask the LORD to bless your plans, and you will
be successful in carrying them out.

Proverbs 16:3 TEV

98

The steps of a good man are ordered by the LORD:
and he delighteth in his way.

Psalm 37:23 KJV

I am always with you; you hold me by my right
hand. You guide me with your counsel, and
afterward you will take me into glory.

Psalm 73:23-24

I will instruct you (says the Lord) and guide you
along the best pathway for your life; I will advise
you and watch your progress.

Psalm 32:8 TLB

Heaven's Port

Henry Ward Beecher was considered by many to be one of the most effective and powerful pulpit orators in the history of the United States. He had a reputation for having a sensitive heart and a great love of the sea. Many of his sermons contained loving anecdotes with a seafaring flavor.

Beecher once said, "Children are the hands by which we take hold of heaven." He had the following to say about a mother's relationship with her child: "A babe is a mother's anchor. She cannot swing far from her moorings. And yet a true mother never lives so little in the present as when by the side of the cradle. Her thoughts follow the imagined future of her child. That babe is the boldest of pilots and guides her fearless thoughts down through scenes of coming years. The old ark never made such voyages as the cradle daily makes."

What a wonderful image to think of a child as being on a voyage from heaven through life to return to heaven's port one day! It is a tremendous challenge and responsibility to educate, prepare, and assist your children as they continue on that voyage. You have an extraordinary opportunity to join them in their journey.[18]

Guidance

This God is our God for ever and ever; he
will be our guide even to the end.

Psalm 48:14

100

The LORD will continually guide you, And satisfy
your desire in scorched places, And give strength to
your bones; And you will be like a watered garden,
And like a spring of water whose waters do not fail.

Isaiah 58:11 NASB

Trust in the LORD with all thine heart; and lean
not unto thine own understanding. In all thy ways
acknowledge him, and he shall direct thy paths.

Proverbs 3:5-6 KJV

Show me your ways, O LORD, teach me your paths;
guide me in your truth and teach me.

Psalm 25:4-5

A Sharp, Square Peg

A mother was helping her son one day with his spelling assignment, and they came to the words *conscious* and *conscience*. She asked her son, "Do you know the difference between these two words?"

He immediately replied, "Sure, Mom. Conscious is when you are aware of something. And conscience is when you wish you weren't."

The conscience is like a sharp, square peg in our hearts. When we are confronted by a situation that calls for a right-or-wrong decision, that square begins to turn. Its corner cuts into our hearts, warning us with an inward "knowing" that we are facing a situation in which we must make a choice against evil and for good.

If the conscience is ignored time after time, however, the corners of the square are gradually worn down, and it becomes a circle that twists and turns at will. When that circle turns within our hearts, there is no inner sensation of warning. In effect, we are left without a conscience.

A sound conscience is truly a gift from God. Teach your children to heed its warning signals early, and they will be spared much pain and heartache.

Happiness

Not that I complain of want; for I have learned,
in whatever state I am, to be content.

Philippians 4:11 RSV

102

To the man who pleases him God gives wisdom
and knowledge and joy.

Ecclesiastes 2:26 RSV

A glad heart makes a cheerful countenance,
but by sorrow of heart the spirit is broken.

Proverbs 15:13 RSV

Happiness or sadness or wealth should not
keep anyone from doing God's work.

I Corinthians 7:30 TLB

Happiness through Giving

Many years ago, a man named David received a new car as a gift from his prosperous brother. One evening as David was leaving work, he noticed a poor child eyeing his shiny new car.

"Is this your car?" the boy asked.

David nodded and said, "My brother gave it to me for Christmas."

The boy said, "It didn't cost you anything? Wow! I wish. . . ." David expected the boy to wish that he had a generous brother, but what the boy said astonished him. He said, "I wish I could be a brother like that." David asked him if he'd like a ride home. The little boy hopped in quickly.

David smiled, thinking that the boy was anxious to show off to his neighbors and family. Again he was wrong. When the two pulled up in front of the boy's house, the boy asked David to wait a minute. He then ran up the steps and soon returned, carrying his crippled brother. David was moved deeply when he heard him say, "There it is, Buddy, just like I told you upstairs. His brother gave it to him. Someday I'm gonna give you one just like it."

This child found his happiness in the joy of giving. What have you taught your children about attaining happiness?

Happiness

Happy is the man that findeth wisdom, and
the man that getteth understanding.

Proverbs 3:13 KJV

104

A generous man will himself be blessed, for
he shares his food with the poor.

Proverbs 22:9

How blessed is the one whom You choose, and
bring near [to You], To dwell in Your courts.

Psalm 65:4 NASB

Do not grieve, for the joy of the LORD is
your strength.

Nehemiah 8:10

Hugs

It's wondrous what a hug can do. A hug can
cheer you when you're blue.

A hug can say, "I love you so," or "I hate to see
you go."

A hug is "Welcome back again," and "Great to
see you! Where've you been?"

A hug can soothe a small child's pain, and bring
a rainbow after rain.

A hug, there's just no doubt about it—we
scarcely could survive without it!

A hug delights and warms and charms. It must
be why God gave us arms.

Hugs are great for fathers and mothers, sweet for
sisters, swell for brothers.

And chances are your favorite aunts love them
more than potted plants.

Kittens crave, puppies love them; heads of state
are not above them.

A hug can break the language barrier, and make
travel so much merrier.

No need to fret about your store of 'em; the
more you give, the more there's more of 'em.

So stretch those arms without delay, and give
someone a hug today!

The fortunate ones grew up with an abundance
of hugs during their childhood years. If you didn't,
you still have an opportunity to institute this
practice in your own home. Open your arms, and
experience happiness![19]

Health

Yes, I will bless the Lord and not forget the glorious things he does for me. He forgives all my sins. He heals me.

Psalm 103:2-3 TLB

106

Surely he took up our infirmities and carried our sorrows, yet we considered him stricken by God, smitten by him, and afflicted. But he was pierced for our transgressions, he was crushed for our iniquities; the punishment that brought us peace was upon him, and by his wounds we are healed.

Isaiah 53:4-5

Ye shall serve the LORD your God, and he shall bless thy bread, and thy water; and I will take sickness away from the midst of thee. There shall nothing cast their young, nor be barren, in thy land: the number of thy days I will fulfil.

Exodus 23:25-26 KJV

Heal me, O LORD, and I shall be healed; save me, and I shall be saved: for thou art my praise.

Jeremiah 17:14 KJV

Standing in the Gap

A young woman lay in a hospital, far from home and family, drifting in and out of consciousness. Several times she became aware of a woman's voice praying for her salvation, as well as for her physical healing. At one point, a physician described her condition as critical, warning those present in the room that she might not survive. Then she heard the same woman speak in faith: "Doctor, I respect what you say, but I cannot accept it. I've been praying, and I believe she will not only recover, but she will walk out of here and live for God."

Before long, the young woman did walk out of that hospital and return to work. It was then she learned that it had been her boss's wife (whom she had met only twice) who had stood in the gap, interceding for her at her hospital bed. When she attempted to thank her for the prayers, the woman replied, "Don't thank me, thank God. Others have prayed for me. Their prayers changed my life."

It was five more years before the young woman gave her life to Christ, but all the while, she never forgot how a persistent woman of God had believed He was faithful to heal.

Teach your children to believe in the healing power of God! Encourage them to pray for healing in their own lives and in the lives of others. Then, remind them to trust in His perfect timing and His unfailing love.

Health

I am the LORD who heals you.

Exodus 15:26 NLT

He spoke the word that healed you, that pulled
you back from the brink of death.

Psalm 107:20 THE MESSAGE

My son, give attention to my words; Incline your
ear to my sayings. For they are life to those who
find them, And health to all their body.

Proverbs 4:20,22 NASB

All the crowd sought to touch him, for power
came forth from him and healed them all.

Luke 6:19 RSV

A Healthy Dose of Words

It may require more energy to say a negative word than a positive one. Research has shown that when we speak positive words—even in difficult circumstances or troubling situations—we become relaxed. As we relax, the flow of blood to the brain increases. A well-oxygenated brain can think more creatively, make wise decisions, find reasonable solutions, and generate pertinent answers.

Positive words also ease relationships and create an atmosphere of peace that is conducive to rest, relaxation, and rejuvenation—all of which are necessary for good health.

On the other hand, a continual flow of negative words causes relationships to suffer, which creates an atmosphere of disharmony and makes for fitful sleep and frayed nerves—none of which are healthy!

Negative thoughts and words also keep the body in a state of tension, constricting muscles and blood vessels, which often causes irrational and uncharacteristic behavior.

God desires for us to walk in the health He has provided for us through the death, burial, and resurrection of Jesus. One of the ways we can do that is to watch what we say. And in order to watch what we say, we must watch what we think. Set a good example for your children by pushing away negative thoughts and thinking positively!

Honesty

Ye shall not steal, neither deal falsely, neither lie one to another.

Leviticus 19:11 KJV

110

That no man go beyond and defraud his brother in any matter: because that the Lord is the avenger of all such, as we also have forewarned you and testified. For God hath not called us unto uncleanness, but unto holiness.

I Thessalonians 4:6-7 KJV

Better *is* a little with righteousness, than great revenues without right.

Proverbs 16:8 KJV

He that walketh righteously, and speaketh uprightly; he that despiseth the gain of oppressions, that shaketh his hands from holding of bribes, that stoppeth his ears from hearing of blood, and shutteth his eyes from seeing evil; He shall dwell on high; his place of defence shall be the munitions of rocks: bread shall be given him; his waters shall be sure.

Isaiah 33:15-16 KJV

The Biggest Bass

Jimmy and his father were fishing early one evening on a lake in upstate New York. It was the day before bass season opened, so they were using worms to catch perch and sunfish. Jimmy decided to practice casting with a small silver lure. The minute the lure hit the water, his pole bent double. Jimmy and his dad knew right away that he had something enormous on the line. A giant moon had risen over the lake by the time he reeled in the biggest fish he had ever seen. There was only one problem—it was a bass!

Jimmy's dad looked at his watch and saw that it was 10 P.M., two hours before bass season opened.

"You'll have to put it back, son," he said.

Jimmy protested, "There'll never be another fish as big as this one!"

He looked around and saw no one else on the water to observe the situation. But he knew by the tone of his father's voice that there would be no discussion. He carefully worked the hook from the bass and lowered it gently back into the water.

Jimmy was right. He has never again seen a bass that big. But he does remember the lesson his dad taught him that night—doing right doesn't mean just when someone is watching! Be sure to teach your children this valuable lesson as well.[20]

Honesty

Lie not one to another, seeing that ye have put off
the old man with his deeds; And have put on the
new man, which is renewed in knowledge after
the image of him that created him.

Colossians 3:9-10 KJV

112

The wicked borroweth, and payeth not again:
but the righteous sheweth mercy, and giveth.

Psalm 37:21 KJV

Withhold not good from them to whom it is due,
when it is in the power of thine hand to do *it*.

Proverbs 3:27 KJV

The integrity of the upright guides them, but the
crookedness of the treacherous destroys them.

Proverbs 11:3 RSV

Telling the Truth

A twelve-year-old boy was the key witness in an important lawsuit. The attorney had put the boy through a rigorous cross-examination and had been unable to shake his concise, damaging testimony. He had given clear answers to all questions that he was asked.

In a stern voice, the attorney asked, "Your father has been telling you how to testify, hasn't he?"

"Yes," said the boy.

"Now," said the attorney with smug satisfaction, "just tell us what your father told you to say."

"Well," replied the boy, "Father told me that the lawyers may try to tangle me, but if I would just be careful and tell the truth, I could say the same thing every time."

This boy's father had taught him an important lesson. Because he followed his father's advice, he was able to give clear testimony in the courtroom.

When we follow our Heavenly Father's lessons from the Bible, we will speak honestly with others in the same way as this young boy. What an example to set for our children![21]

Jealousy

When his brothers saw that their father loved him more than all his brothers, they hated him, and could not speak peaceably to him. Now Joseph had a dream, and when he told it to his brothers they only hated him the more.

Genesis 37:4-5 RSV

Don't hold grudges. . . . Stop being angry and don't try to take revenge. I am the LORD, and I command you to love others as much as you love yourself.

Leviticus 19:17-18 CEV

Do not fret because of evil men or be envious of those who do wrong.

Psalm 37:1

They began to argue among themselves as to who would be the greatest in the coming Kingdom. Jesus told them, "In this world the kings and great men order their people around, and yet they are called 'friends of the people.' But among you, those who are the greatest should take the lowest rank, and the leader should be like a servant.

Luke 22:24-26 NLT

Blind Jealousy and Blind Justice

A wealthy man died, apparently without leaving a will. According to law, his estate was divided among surviving relatives through a public auction.

During the auction, three distant cousins who had fought for years began to bid, often competing with each other. This only drove up the price.

Toward the end, the auctioneer held up a dusty framed photograph, but no one bid on it. Finally a woman approached the auctioneer and asked if she could buy it for a dollar, which was all she had. She said she had been a servant of the wealthy man and recognized the picture—it was of the deceased man's only son who had died trying to rescue a drowning child.

The auctioneer accepted the dollar, and the woman went home and started to place the photograph on a table beside her bed. Then she noticed a bulge in the back of the frame. She undid the backing, and there, to her amazement, was the rich man's will.

His instructions were simple: "I bequeath all my possessions to whomever cares enough for my son to cherish this photograph."

Often times, jealousy can blind us to what truly matters in life, so train your children to look beyond their own selfish desires. Teach them instead to place the needs of others before their own.

Jealousy

Love is patient, love is kind. It does not envy, it does not boast, it is not proud.

1 Corinthians 13:4

You shall not covet.

Exodus 20:17 NKJV

Wrath is fierce and anger is a flood, But who can stand before jealousy?

Proverbs 27:4 NASB

Where you have envy and selfish ambition, there you find disorder and every evil practice.

James 3:16

Focus on What You Have

*G*ood Morning America former co-host Joan Lunden recalls:

When I first came on [the] program in 1978, hosting with David Hartman, he got to interview all the celebrities and politicians and kings. I got the information spots. . . . I received piles of letters from women who were unhappy that I was allowing myself to be used in this way. Well, the fact was I enjoyed those spots and I was good at them. I had to accept that it was either that way or no way at all.

I can't see any reason to spend your time frustrated, angry, or upset about things you don't have or you can't have or you can't yet do. I drill this into my children when I hear them say, "I don't have this." I'll say, "Don't focus on what you don't have. Focus on what you do have and be grateful for it. Be proud of what you can do. Those things you can't do yet, maybe you will do."

When we are jealous of others who have gifts and talents that we don't, we get nowhere. Remind your children that God will never ask them to become something that they aren't; all He will ask is that they use the gifts He's given them to the best of their ability.

Joy

Ye shall go out with joy, and be led forth with peace: the mountains and the hills shall break forth before you into singing, and all the trees of the field shall clap their hands.

Isaiah 55:12 KJV

118

Blessed is the people that know the joyful sound: they shall walk, O LORD, in the light of thy countenance. In thy name shall they rejoice all the day: and in thy righteousness shall they be exalted.

Psalm 89:15-16 KJV

The voice of rejoicing and salvation is in the tabernacles of the righteous: the right hand of the LORD doeth valiantly.

Psalm 118:15 KJV

"These things have I spoken unto you, that my joy might remain in you, and that your joy might be full."

John 15:11 KJV

Wasn't That Dad?

A family planned a vacation to the West Coast one summer. All the plans were made, but at the last minute Dad couldn't go because he had to complete some work that had been delayed. Mom insisted she could do the driving. Dad helped plan their route and made the reservations where they would stop each night.

After two weeks, Dad was able to complete his work and decided to surprise his family. Without calling them, he flew to a city on their route, took a taxi out of the city, and asked to be let out along the highway. According to his travel plan for the family, they would be driving along this same highway later in the day. When he saw the family car, he stuck out his thumb like a hitchhiker. As Mom and the children drove past, one of the children yelled, "Mom, wasn't that Dad?" The car came to a screeching halt, and the family enjoyed a wonderful reunion.

A reporter later asked the father why he did such a crazy thing. He said, "After I die, I want my kids to be able to say, 'Dad sure was fun, wasn't he?'"

Joyful times cause your children to flourish and allow guidance and discipline to seep in.[22]

Joy

Thou hast put gladness in my heart.

Psalm 4:7 KJV

120

They that sow in tears shall reap in joy. He that goeth forth and weepeth, bearing precious seed, shall doubtless come again with rejoicing, bringing his sheaves with him.

Psalm 126:5-6 KJV

I will rejoice in the LORD, I will joy in the God of my salvation.

Habakkuk 3:18 KJV

For our heart shall rejoice in him, because we have trusted in his holy name.

Psalm 33:21 KJV

The Joy of a Child

What are children? They are bundles of energy who stop running around and asking questions only when they are totally exhausted and drop off to sleep. They climb trees, dig around in streams, and generally leave adults frazzled just watching them. Some are quieter than others, but they all ask questions. It does not matter to the child if this drives you to distraction or puts a big smile on your face. They "question" and "do" day in and day out.

Children behave this way because they want to know. They are like enormous dry sponges, soaking up everything around them. It is a priceless moment when they see something special. Their faces light up like Christmas morning. Their eyes bulge open and mouths gape almost in disbelief, and then they smile. We adults have often forgotten how to smile.

Children don't hide a thing. If they are excited or scared, it is obvious. They accept and return love and care with reckless abandon. We may put away childish thinking, but there is a reward in experiencing the joy of a child.[23]

Knowledge

Praise God forever and ever, because he has
wisdom and power. . . . He gives wisdom to
those who are wise and knowledge to those
who understand.

Daniel 2:20-21 NCV

Wisdom and knowledge will be the stability of
your times, And the strength of salvation.

Isaiah 33:6 NKJV

O the depth of the riches both of the wisdom
and knowledge of God! how unsearchable are
his judgments, and his ways past finding out!

Romans 11:33 KJV

Wisdom will enter your heart, And knowledge
will be pleasant to your soul.

Proverbs 2:10 NASB

122

The Best Five Years

The importance of the first few years of a child's life cannot be overemphasized. It is during those years that the foundation is laid for a child's language ability, ethics, morality, and value systems. In his book, *All Men Are Brothers*, Mahatma Gandhi said this about the instilling of values in very early childhood: "I am convinced that for the proper upbringing of children, the parents ought to have a general knowledge of the care and nursing of babies. We labour under a sort of superstition that the child has nothing to learn during the first five years of his or her life. On the contrary, the fact is that the child never learns in after life what it does in his or her first five years. The education of the child begins with conception."

The famous psychoanalyst Sigmund Freud agreed. A Viennese woman once asked him, "How early should I begin the education of my child?"

Freud responded with a question of his own, "When will the child be born?"

"Born?" the woman asked. "Why, he is already five years old!"

"My goodness, woman," Freud cried, "don't stand there talking to me–hurry home! You have already wasted the best five years!"

Lay a strong foundation for your children during their impressionable younger years. Don't waste the precious time God has given you to impact their lives and turn them toward Him.[24]

Knowledge

A man of understanding and knowledge
maintains order.

Proverbs 28:2

124

The fear of the LORD is the beginning of wisdom,
and knowledge of the Holy One is understanding.

Proverbs 9:10

If I have the gift of prophecy and can fathom all
mysteries and all knowledge, and if I have a faith
that can move mountains, but have not love,
I am nothing.

1 Corinthians 13:2

Grow in the grace and knowledge of our Lord
and Savior Jesus Christ.

2 Peter 3:18 NASB

Real-Life Practice

A mother and father helped their oldest son pack his belongings and prepare for his first year of college. The parents had provided their son with every conceivable item that he might need to begin living independently. They also gave him his first checkbook with the funds deposited into the account to pay his beginning college expenses. Two months later, bank overdrafts on the son's account began arriving at the parents' home.

"How are things at school?" Dad asked in a phone call to his son.

"Just great, Dad," his son replied.

"John," his dad responded, "you've written over $500 in checks when there was only $10 left in your checking account. You are extensively overdrawn."

"But that can't be," argued John, "I still have several checks left in my checkbook."

Parents often assume that their children have learned a necessary skill at school, when the reality is, they haven't. They may have been exposed to the information at some point but did not receive any real-life practice to make it a part of their knowledge. Make it a point to teach your children how to balance a checkbook, do the laundry, and comparison shop for groceries. They'll thank you for it later![25]

Laughter

There is a time for everything, and a season for every activity under heaven: . . . a time to weep and a time to laugh, a time to mourn and a time to dance.

Ecclesiastes 3:1,4

126

Abraham fell upon his face, and laughed, and said in his heart, Shall a child be born unto him that is an hundred years old? And shall Sarah, that is ninety years old, bear?

Genesis 17:17 KJV

Our mouths were filled with laughter, our tongues with songs of joy.

Psalm 126:2

"Blessed are you who hunger now, for you will be satisfied. Blessed are you who weep now, for you will laugh."

Luke 6:21

Living in the Moment

On a recent canoe trip to North Carolina, one man was strengthened and lifted up by the childlike joy of a wonderful moment. The following is how he recorded it in his journal:

> Somewhere near the beginning of my river run . . . I heard behind me a joyous tumult of laughter from an oncoming raft . . . I turned just in time to see a large raft filled to overflowing with madly paddling youngsters, all of them in full-throated laughter. It was a raft full of Down's syndrome kids out for a day on the river. Truly uninhibited joy that is rarely seen except in tiny children was erupting in their voices and on their faces. They were feeding upon the moment with such abandon that all else was swept away. Their whole focus, their whole life was right here. Right now. And the power of it was unconquerable, sweeping up everything within the sound of their voices into an all-encompassing joy. "Thank you!" I shouted and raised my paddle high in salute to their joy and grace. And wisdom.

Children live in the events of the moment, spontaneously expressing their joy and delight. They don't let thoughts of tomorrow interfere with that joy. Remember to laugh with your children today![26]

Laughter

Sarah said, God hath made me to laugh, so that all that hear will laugh with me.

Genesis 21:6 KJV

128

He will yet fill your mouth with laughter and your lips with shouts of joy.

Job 8:21

God said to Abraham, "Why did Sarah laugh? Why did she say 'Can an old woman like me have a baby?' Is anything too hard for God?

Genesis 18:13-14 TLB

A merry heart doeth good like a medicine: but a broken spirit drieth the bones.

Proverbs 17:22 KJV

Divine Medicine

The great evangelist D. L. Moody was a man of wholesome humor and an occasional practical joke. He sometimes told stories with such enthusiasm that he would laugh until he cried. He enjoyed gathering his associates about him at the close of the day to see who could tell the best stories. When someone asked him how he could laugh so fully after preaching so seriously, he answered, "If I didn't laugh, I would have a nervous breakdown at the pace at which I live."

Leslie B. Flynn wrote, "Though people know about the prodigious labors of David Livingstone in opening up Africa for missionary endeavor, few know that in the midst of their lonely life, he and his wife often acted like jolly school kids on an excursion. Mirth saturated their lives so much that Livingstone more than once said to his wife, 'Really, my dear, we ought not to indulge in so many jokes. We are getting too old. It is not becoming. We must be more staid.'"

Teach your children that appropriate humor is like divine medicine. It cheers the mind, enlightens the message, and relieves the listener.

Give us, Lord,
A bit of sun,
A bit of work,
And a bit of fun.[27]

Love

The fruit of the Spirit is love, joy, peace,
longsuffering, gentleness, goodness, faith.

Galatians 5:22 KJV

130

Above all, love each other deeply, because love
covers over a multitude of sins.

1 Peter 4:8

Whoever loves is a child of God and knows God.
Whoever does not love does not know God,
for God is love.

1 John 4:7-8 TEV

I have loved you with an everlasting love;
Therefore I have drawn you with lovingkindness.

Jeremiah 31:3 NASB

Love Unlimited

Karl Menninger once said, "Love cures people—both the ones who give it and the ones who receive it." He organized the work of the Menninger Clinic around love. "From the top psychiatrist down to the electricians and caregivers," Menninger said, "all contacts with patients must manifest love." And it was "love unlimited." The result was that hospitalization time was cut in half.

One of the patients at the clinic was a woman who sat in her rocking chair for three years and never said a word to anyone. Her doctor called a nurse and said, "Mary, I'm giving you Mrs. Brown as your patient. All I'm asking you to do is to love her till she gets well." The nurse tried it. She got a rocking chair of the same kind as Mrs. Brown's, sat beside her, and loved her morning, noon, and night. On the third day, Mrs. Brown spoke. Within a week, she was out of her shell—and healthy.

Research projects have been done to ascertain the bonding that develops between a mother and her child in the first months after childbirth. Studies have shown that babies deprived of touch and their mothers' voices develop at a slower rate than those held and spoken to. God did not mean for us to grow up in a vacuum. Hug the members of your family daily—both children and adults. We all need love![28]

Love

We need have no fear of someone who loves us perfectly; his perfect love for us eliminates all dread.

1 John 4:18 TLB

132

"Love your enemies, do good, and lend, hoping for nothing in return; and your reward will be great."

Luke 6:35 NKJV

"This is my commandment, That ye love one another, as I have loved you."

John 15:12 KJV

Those who do not love their brothers and sisters, whom they have seen, cannot love God, whom they have never seen.

1 John 4:20 NCV

All They Did

There was once a little boy who was given everything he wanted. As an infant, he was given a bottle at the first little whimper. He was picked up and held whenever he fussed. His parents said, "He'll think we don't love him if we let him cry."

He was never disciplined for leaving the yard. He suffered no consequences for breaking windows or tearing up flowerbeds. His parents said, "He'll think we don't love him if we stifle his will."

His mother picked up after him and made his bed. His parents said, "He'll think we don't love him if we give him chores."

Nobody ever stopped him from using bad words. He was never reprimanded for scribbling on his bedroom wall. His parents said, "He'll think we don't love him if we stifle his creativity."

He was never required to go to Sunday school. His parents said, "He'll think we don't love him if we force religion down his throat."

One day the parents received news that their son was in jail on a felony charge. They cried to each other, "All we ever did was love and do for him." Unfortunately, that is, indeed, all they did.

Children need boundaries to feel loved. The key is consistency.[29]

Marriage

Let thy fountain be blessed: and rejoice with the wife of thy youth. Let her be as the loving hind and pleasant roe; let her breasts satisfy thee at all times; and be thou ravished always with her love.

Proverbs 5:18-19 KJV

134

There are three things that amaze me—no, four things I do not understand: how an eagle glides through the sky, how a snake slithers on a rock, how a ship navigates the ocean, how a man loves a woman.

Proverbs 30:18-19 NLT

A wife of noble character who can find? She is worth far more than rubies. Her husband has full confidence in her and lacks nothing of value.

Proverbs 31:10-11

She opens her mouth with wisdom, and the teaching of kindness is on her tongue. She looks well to the ways of her household, and does not eat the bread of idleness. Her children rise up and call her blessed; her husband also, and he praises her: "Many women have done excellently, but you surpass them all."

Proverbs 31:26-29 RSV

Killing (and Kindling) with Kindness

Pete sat down with the divorce lawyer. He told such a tale of woe: His wife was a total bore. She always looked a mess, the house was worse, and all she did was complain, especially about him. Now he wanted to make her as miserable as she made him.

"Pete," the lawyer said, "I've got the perfect plan. Go home now, and start treating your wife like a royalty. Bring her roses. Take her out for dinner. Tell her how beautiful she looks. And then, just when she's getting used to this treatment, pack your bags. I promise you, nothing will devastate her more."

Pete thought it was a fantastic idea. He couldn't wait to start hatching the plot. He helped her around the house, gave her breakfast in bed, took her on weekend getaways, and showered her with compliments.

After three weeks, the lawyer called. "I've got the divorce papers ready," he said. "I can make you a free man anytime."

"Are you kidding?" Pete cried. "You wouldn't believe the changes she's made. I'm married to an absolute queen. I wouldn't divorce her in a million years."

Provide your children the Godly example of a loving marriage relationship. Place your spouse's needs before your own, and constantly strive to rekindle your love for each other.

Marriage

Be subject to one another out of reverence for Christ.

Ephesians 5:21 RSV

136

Wives, submit to your husbands as to the Lord.

Ephesians 5:22

You husbands must love your wives with the same love Christ showed the church. He gave up his life for her.

Ephesians 5:25 NLT

As the Scriptures say, "A man leaves his father and mother to get married, and he becomes like one person with his wife."

Ephesians 5:31 CEV

Age before Beauty

From German pastor and theologian Helmut Thielicke comes this beautiful picture of a marriage where love has continued to grow all through the years:

I once knew a very old married couple who radiated a profound happiness. The wife, especially, who was almost unable to move because of her age and illness, possessed a kind face etched with a hundred lines by the joys and sufferings of many years. She exhibited such a gratitude for life that I was touched to the quick.

I asked myself what could possibly be the source of this kindly person's radiance. In so many respects they were quite ordinary people, and their home indicated only the most modest comforts.

Suddenly I saw where it all came from. I saw these two speaking to each other, and their eyes hanging upon each other. It became clear to me that this woman was dearly loved.

It was not that she was loved all those years by her husband because she was a cheerful and pleasant person. It was the other way around. Because she was so loved, she became the person I saw before me.

In your marriage, you can enjoy a lifelong relationship with your beloved. Let it be a Godly relationship that enhances not only your own lives, but your children's lives as well.

Money/Materialism

The love of money is a root of all kinds of evil, for which some have strayed from the faith in their greediness, and pierced themselves through with many sorrows.

1 Timothy 6:10 NKJV

138

Give me an eagerness for your decrees; do not inflict me with love for money!

Psalm 119:36 NLT

Wisdom is a shelter as money is a shelter, but the advantage of knowledge is this: that wisdom preserves the life of its possessor.

Ecclesiastes 7:12

Instruct those who are rich in this present world not to be conceited or to fix their hope on the uncertainty of riches, but on God, who richly supplies us with all things to enjoy.

1 Timothy 6:17 NASB

Money, Money, Money

In 1923, eight of the most powerful money magnates in the world gathered for a meeting at the Edgewater Beach Hotel in Chicago, Illinois. The combined resources and assets of these eight men tallied more than the U.S. Treasury that year. In the group were the following men: Charles Schwab, president of a steel company; Richard Whitney, president of the New York Stock Exchange; Arthur Cutton, a wheat speculator; Albert Fall, a presidential cabinet member and a personally wealthy man; Jesse Livermore, the greatest Wall Street "bear" in his generation; Leon Fraser, president of the International Bank of Settlements; and Ivan Krueger, head of the largest monopoly in the nation. What an impressive gathering of financial eagles!

What happened to these men in later years? Schwab died penniless. Whitney served a life sentence in Sing Sing prison. Cutton became insolvent. Fall was pardoned from a federal prison so he might die at home. Fraser, Livermore, and Krueger committed suicide. Seven of these eight extremely rich men ended their lives with nothing.

Teach your children that money is certainly not the answer to life's ills! Only God can give us peace, happiness, and joy. When we focus on God and His goodness, we can live contentedly, knowing that God will meet all our needs.

Money/Materialism

"Don't store up treasures here on earth where they can erode away or may be stolen. Store them in heaven where they will never lose their value."

Matthew 6:19-20 TLB

140

Stay away from the love of money; be satisfied with what you have.

Hebrews 13:5 NLT

"Be careful and guard against all kinds of greed. Life is not measured by how much one owns."

Luke 12:15 NCV

"No one can serve two masters. Either he will hate the one and love the other, or he will be devoted to the one and despise the other. You cannot serve both God and Money."

Matthew 6:24

Just to Stretch His Soul

R. Lee Sharpe of Carrollton, Georgia, tells an interesting story that was published in the *Alabama Baptist*.

"I was just a kid," related Mr. Sharpe. "One spring day, Father called me to go with him to old man Trussell's blacksmith shop. He had left a rake and a hoe to be repaired. And there they were, ready, fixed like new. Father handed over a silver dollar for the repairing, but Mr. Trussell refused to take it. 'No,' he said, 'there's no charge for that little job.' But father insisted that he take the pay.

"If I live a thousand years," said Mr. Sharpe, "I'll never forget that great blacksmith's reply, 'Sid,' he said to my father, 'can't you let a man do something now and then just to stretch his soul?'

"It is the old law. The giver receives a reward. Bread cast upon the waters comes back. One who stretches his or her soul in deeds of love and kindness, unfailingly reaps a just reward."

Henry van Dyke once said, "We make a living by what we get, but we make a life by what we give." Teach your children that life here on earth is a training place for all eternity.[30]

Obedience

If you listen to these regulations and obey them
faithfully, the LORD your God will keep his
covenant of unfailing love with you, as he
solemnly promised your ancestors.

Deuteronomy 7:12 NLT

142

"If you keep my commands, you'll remain
intimately at home in my love. That's what
I've done—kept my Father's commands and
made myself at home in his love."

John 15:10 THE MESSAGE

When we obey God, we are sure that we know
him. We truly love God only when we obey him
as we should, and then we know that we belong
to him.

1 John 2:3,5 CEV

Dear friends, if our hearts do not condemn us, we
have confidence before God and receive from him
anything we ask, because we obey his commands
and do what pleases him.

1 John 3:21-22

Obeying God's Call

In *Dakota*, Kathleen Norris writes:

A Benedictine sister from the Philippines once told me what her community did when some sisters took to the streets in the popular revolt against the Marcos regime. Some did not think it proper for nuns to demonstrate in public, let alone risk arrest. In a group meeting that began and ended with prayer, the sisters who wished to continue demonstrating explained that this was for them a religious obligation; those who disapproved also had their say. Everyone spoke; everyone heard and gave counsel.

It was eventually decided that the nuns who were demonstrating should continue to do so; those who wished to express solidarity but were unable to march would prepare food and provide medical assistance to the demonstrators, and those who disapproved would pray for everyone. The sisters laughed and said, "If one of the conservative sisters was praying that we young, crazy ones would come to our senses and stay off the streets, that was okay. We were still a community."

God calls some to action, others to support, and still others to pray. Encourage your children to be confident in their calling. Each will be doing what is "right" in His eyes if they obey His call!

Obedience

To obey is better than sacrifice, and to hearken than the fat of rams.

1 Samuel 15:22 KJV

144

If they obey and serve him, they will spend the rest of their days in prosperity and their years in contentment.

Job 36:11

"He who has my commandments and keeps them, he it is who loves me; and he who loves me will be loved by my Father, and I will love him and manifest myself to him."

John 14:21 RSV

The world and all its wanting, wanting, wanting is on the way out—but whoever does what God wants is set for eternity.

1 John 2:17 THE MESSAGE

Chickens

*J*ack London's wonderful classic, *White Fang,* tells the story of an animal, half-dog half-wolf, as he survives his life in the wild and then learns to live among men.

White Fang was very fond of chickens and on one occasion raided a chicken-roost and killed fifty hens. His master scolded him and then took him into the chicken yard. When White Fang saw his favorite food walking around right in front of him, he obeyed his natural impulse and lunged for a chicken. He was immediately checked by his master's voice. They stayed in the chicken yard for quite a while, and every time White Fang made a move toward a chicken, his master's voice would stop him. In this way he learned what his master wanted—he had learned to ignore the chickens.

Out of love and a desire to obey his master's will, White Fang overcame his natural, inborn desires. He may not have understood the reason, but he chose to bend his will to his master's.

In a similar fashion, instruct your children that their lives will always be full of "chickens." Encourage them to decide in advance to serve their Master and to bend their will to His.

Patience

Be patient and wait for the LORD to act; don't be worried about those who prosper or those who succeed in their evil plans.

Psalm 37:7 TEV

146

It is better to be patient than to be proud. Don't become angry quickly, because getting angry is foolish.

Ecclesiastes 7:8-9 NCV

When the Holy Spirit controls our lives he will produce this kind of fruit in us: love, joy, peace, patience, kindness, goodness, faithfulness.

Galatians 5:22 TLB

Be completely humble and gentle; be patient, bearing with one another in love.

Ephesians 4:2

Little Monica

A man noticed a woman in the grocery store with a three-year-old girl in her basket. As they passed the cookie section, the little girl asked for cookies, and her mother told her no. The little girl started to whine and fuss, and the mother said quietly, "Now, Monica, don't be upset. We just have half the aisles left to go through. It won't be long."

Soon they came to the candy aisle, where the little girl began to shout for candy. When told she couldn't have any, she began to scream. The mother said, "There, there, Monica, don't cry— only two more aisles to go, and then we'll be checking out."

When they got to the checkout stand, the little girl immediately clamored for gum. She burst into a terrible tantrum upon discovering there'd be no gum purchased. The mother patiently said, "Monica, we'll be through this checkout stand in five minutes, and then you can go home and have a nice nap."

The man followed them out to the parking lot and stopped the woman to commend her. "I couldn't help noticing how patient you were with little Monica," he said.

At that time the mother said, "I'm Monica. My little girl's name is Tammy."

Sometimes the only way to make it through the day is to talk yourself through it![31]

Patience

I waited patiently for the LORD to help me, and he turned to me and heard my cry.

Psalm 40:1 NLT

148

Let us lay aside every weight, and the sin which doth so easily beset us, and let us run with patience the race that is set before us.

Hebrews 12:1 KJV

Warn those who are unruly, comfort the fainthearted, uphold the weak, be patient with all.

1 Thessalonians 5:14 NKJV

A man's wisdom gives him patience.

Proverbs 19:11

A Soft Question

Carolyn Hagan wrote an article in *Child* magazine that contained an interview with Pulitzer Prize-winning author Alice Walker. A portion of her story follows:

"When I was a little girl, I accidentally broke a fruit jar. Several brothers and a sister were nearby who could have done it. But my father turned to me and asked, 'Did you break the jar, Alice?'

"Looking into his large, brown eyes, I knew he wanted me to tell the truth. I also knew he might punish me if I did. But the truth inside of me wanted badly to be expressed. 'I broke the jar,' I said.

"The love in his eyes rewarded and embraced me. Suddenly I felt an inner peace that I still recall with gratitude to this day."

This was a parent who knew the value of patience in interacting with his children. He didn't yell and scream; he asked the question softly, hoping for the truth. Wonderful results occur when you discipline your children consistently and patiently. If you haven't tried this approach with your children, it might bring you unexpected joy in your relationship with them.[32]

Peace

Great peace have they who love your law, and
nothing can make them stumble.

Psalm 119:165

150

LORD, You will establish peace for us, Since
You have also performed for us all our works.

Isaiah 26:12 NASB

Be perfect, be of good comfort, be of one mind,
live in peace; and the God of love and peace shall
be with you.

2 Corinthians 13:11 KJV

When a man's ways are pleasing to the LORD, He
makes even his enemies to be at peace with him.

Proverbs 16:7 NASB

Love Your Enemies

When Rosa Parks was arrested for sitting in the front of a bus in an area reserved for white passengers, the black people of Montgomery, Alabama, were angry. It was 1955, and segregation regarding public transportation, restrooms, drinking fountains, and other areas was rampant throughout the South.

The twenty-seven-year-old minister of the Dexter Avenue Baptist Church in Montgomery met with other ministers to decide on a course of action. They urged their fellow blacks not to ride the city's buses on December 5. However, the bus boycott lasted 382 days. The ministers repeatedly asked their congregations to remain peaceful and calm.

The young minister Martin Luther King Jr. was made famous internationally by the publicity surrounding the bus boycott. He became, not only a spokesman for his community, but a target as well. A bomb exploded on his front porch. Although no one was injured, a crowd of more than a thousand people gathered in anger. King spoke from the smoking ruins of his porch, saying, "Be peaceful. I want you to love your enemies."

Martin Luther King Jr. was a man of deep convictions who did not waver in the face of hostility. First and foremost, he was a man of God. In like manner, teach your children to sink their roots deeply into the soil of God's Word. It will strengthen them for the challenges of life.[33]

Peace

Turn your back on sin; do something good.
Embrace peace—don't let it get away!

Psalm 34:14 THE MESSAGE

152

Therefore, since we have been made right in God's
sight by faith, we have peace with God because of
what Jesus Christ our Lord has done for us.

Romans 5:1 NLT

May the God of hope fill you with all joy and peace
as you trust in him, so that you may overflow with
hope by the power of the Holy Spirit.

Romans 15:13

The meek shall inherit the earth; and shall delight
themselves in the abundance of peace.

Psalm 37:11 KJV

Peacemakers

Mahatma Gandhi is a man who had a clearly defined value system, one rooted in peace.

Gandhi founded his campaign of nonviolent civil disobedience on the term *satyagraha*, which means "a force born of truth and love." Even when his followers were fired upon by the British, Gandhi condemned any form of violence in retaliation. He was arrested and imprisoned repeatedly, but always released. He gained control of his nation without firing a shot.

153

Gandhi accomplished his goals, not only by means of moral pressure, but through a thorough knowledge of British law and culture. In essence, Gandhi said to the English, "I believe in your legal system, and I believe it is rooted in values that are higher than your methods."

Teach your children to be peacemakers, not by avoiding conflict, but by dealing kindly and respectfully with others and refusing to retaliate in anger. In so doing, you will be endowing them with the ability to live in peace and encouraging them to uncover the gifts that lie within them. In essence, you will be teaching them to please God and bless others.[34]

Perseverance

154

Consider it pure joy, my brothers, whenever you
face trials of many kinds, because you know that
the testing of your faith develops perseverance.
Perseverance must finish its work so that you may
be mature and complete, not lacking anything.

James 1:2-4

May the Master take you by the hand and
lead you along the path of God's love and
Christ's endurance.

2 Thessalonians 3:5 THE MESSAGE

Love bears up under anything and everything that
comes, is ever ready to believe the best of every
person, its hopes are fadeless under all circumstances,
and it endures everything [without weakening].

1 Corinthians 13:7 AMP

If [anyone suffers] as a Christian, he is not to be
ashamed, but is to glorify God in this name.

1 Peter 4:16 NASB

Two Thousand Ways
It Can't Be Done

Many times Thomas Edison failed the first or second or tenth time in his attempts to discover something new, but he didn't mind. He just kept on trying! It is said that he made thousands upon thousands of attempts before he got his famous electric light to operate.

One day a workman to whom he had given a task came to him and said, "Mr. Edison, it cannot be done."

"How often have you tried?" asked Edison.

"About two thousand times," replied the man.

"Then go back and try it two thousand more times," said Edison. "You have only found out that there are two thousand ways in which it cannot be done."

This story reveals one of the great truths of life. Keep trying until you get it right! Sometimes our pessimism or ego or pride or just plain laziness gets in the way of the things we want to accomplish. Think of it in Edison's terminology—you've only found out how many ways it can't be done.

Set a good example for your children by tackling life's roadblocks with a positive attitude.[35]

Perseverance

We also glory in tribulations, knowing that
tribulation produces perseverance; and
perseverance, character; and character, hope.

Romans 5:3-4 NKJV

156

You need to persevere so that when you have
done the will of God, you will receive what
he has promised.

Hebrews 10:36

"The good soil represents honest, good-hearted
people who hear God's message, cling to it, and
steadily produce a huge harvest."

Luke 8:15 NLT

Pray at all times in the Spirit, with all prayer
and supplication. To that end keep alert with all
perseverance, making supplication for all the saints.

Ephesians 6:18 RSV

The Most Frightened Man in America

Thomas J. Watson Jr. writes in *Father, Son & Co.: My Life at IBM and Beyond* about his first few days as CEO: "When my father died in 1956—six weeks after making me head of IBM—I was the most frightened man in America. For ten years he had groomed me to succeed him, and I had been the young man in a hurry, eager to take over, cocky, and impatient. Now, suddenly, I had the job. But what I didn't have was Dad there to back me up."

Watson admits that he "didn't have much motivation as a youth." He spent so much time flying airplanes at Brown University that he barely graduated. However, his father continued to encourage him. He said, "At some point, something will catch hold, and you are going to be a great man."

Watson returned home after World War II "confident, for the first time that I might be capable of running IBM." During his fifteen years as head of IBM, the company entered the computer era and grew more than tenfold. He says of the success, "I think I was at least successful enough that people could say I was the worthy son of a worthy father."

Continually encourage your children to fulfill God's plan for their lives.[36]

Prayer

"When you pray, go away by yourself, all alone, and shut the door behind you and pray to your Father secretly, and your Father, who knows your secrets, will reward you."

Matthew 6:6 TLB

158

Even before they finish praying to me, I will answer their prayers.

Isaiah 65:24 TEV

"Believe that you have received the things you ask for in prayer, and God will give them to you."

Mark 11:24 NCV

The earnest prayer of a righteous person has great power and wonderful results.

James 5:16 NLT

The Heart-Maker

"You must have a good heart," one man said to his child, "if you are going to act right in this world." He continued, "Suppose my watch was not keeping time very well. Would it do any good if I went to the town clock and made the hands of my watch point exactly the same as those of the larger clock in the square? No, of course not! Rather, I should take my watch to a watchmaker or jewelry store that repairs watches. It is only when my watch has been cleaned and repaired that its hands will be able to keep time accurately all day long."

When we spend time in prayer, we are going to the Heart-Maker, asking Him to clean and repair our hearts from the damage caused by the wrong things we have done. We are asking Him to put us right again on the inside so that we can more clearly determine right from wrong.

When our children see us in prayer, they are much more likely to go to God when they feel their own lives are in turmoil, rather than turning to the world and resetting their souls according to its standards and priorities.[37]

Prayer

The eyes of the Lord watch over those who do right, and his ears are open to their prayers.

1 Peter 3:12 NLT

160

"When you are praying, if you are angry with someone, forgive him so that your Father in heaven will also forgive your sins."

Mark 11:25 NCV

Call unto me, and I will answer thee, and shew thee great and mighty things, which thou knowest not.

Jeremiah 33:3 KJV

When good people pray, the LORD listens.

Proverbs 15:29 TEV

A Father Only Builds

General Douglas MacArthur once said, "By profession I am a soldier and take pride in that fact. But I am more proud, infinitely more, to be a father. A soldier destroys in order to build; a father only builds, never destroys. The one has the potentialities of death; the other embodies creation and life. While the hordes of death are mighty, the battalions of life are mightier still. It is my hope that my son, when I am gone, will remember me not from the battles, but in the home, repeating with him our simple daily prayer, 'Our Father, who art in Heaven.'"

These words by General MacArthur reflect his priorities in life. Parents who give their children the example of prayer provide for them a foundation upon which to base all their decisions.

Prayer is not difficult. What is difficult is living without God's presence beside you daily, both during the good times and the bad. Talk to Him throughout the day just as you would a good friend, which indeed He is. God doesn't ask for big words or rehearsed speeches; He wants to hear what is in your heart.[38]

Protection

You have done so much for those who come to you for protection.

Psalm 31:19 NLT

162

When you pass through the waters, I will be with you; And through the rivers, they will not overflow you. When you walk through the fire, you will not be scorched, Nor will the flame burn you.

Isaiah 43:2 NASB

The eyes of the LORD run to and fro throughout the whole earth, to show Himself strong on behalf of those whose heart is loyal to Him.

2 Chronicles 16:9 NKJV

The Lord is faithful, and he will strengthen and protect you from the evil one.

2 Thessalonians 3:3

No Oars

There is a story about an English steamer that was wrecked on a rocky coast many years ago. Twelve women set out into the dark stormy waters in a lifeboat, and the turbulent sea immediately carried them away from the wreckage. Having no oars, they were at the mercy of the wind and the waves. They spent a fearful night being tossed about by the raging storm.

They probably would have lost all hope if it had not been for the spiritual stamina of one woman who calmly prayed aloud for divine protection. Then urging her companions to put their trust in the Lord, she encouraged them by singing hymns of comfort.

Throughout the dark hours, her voice rang out across the water. Early the next morning, a small craft came searching for survivors. The man at the helm would have missed the women in the fog if he had not heard a woman singing the selection from *Elijah* "Oh, rest in the Lord, wait patiently for Him!" Steering in the direction of her strong voice, he soon spotted the drifting lifeboat. While many others were lost that night, these trusting few were rescued.

Teach your children to trust in God![39]

Protection

He orders his angels to protect you wherever you go.

Psalm 91:11 NLT

The LORD thy God in the midst of thee is mighty; he will save, he will rejoice over thee with joy.

Zephaniah 3:17 KJV

He protects those who are loyal to him, but evil people will be silenced in darkness. Power is not the key to success.

1 Samuel 2:9 NCV

Let all who take refuge in you be glad; let them ever sing for joy. Spread your protection over them, that those who love your name may rejoice in you.

Psalm 5:11

A Real Traffic-Stopper

While driving along the freeway, the adults in the front seat of a car were talking when suddenly, they heard the horrifying sound of a car door opening, the whistle of wind, and a sickening thud. They quickly turned and saw that the three-year-old child riding in the back seat had fallen out of the car and was tumbling along the freeway. The driver screeched to a stop and then raced back toward her child. To her surprise, she found that all the traffic had stopped just a few feet away from her child. Her daughter had not been hit.

A truck driver drove the girl to a nearby hospital. The doctors there rushed her into the emergency room and soon came back with the good news: other than a few scrapes and bruises, the girl was fine—no broken bones, no apparent internal damage.

As the mother rushed to her child, the little girl opened her eyes and said, "Mommy, you know I wasn't afraid. While I was lying on the road waiting for you to get back to me, I looked up, and right there I saw Jesus holding back the traffic with His arms out."[40]

Reconciliation

Pursue peace with all people, and holiness, without which no one will see the Lord: looking carefully lest anyone fall short of the grace of God; lest any root of bitterness springing up cause trouble, and by this many become defiled.

Hebrews 12:14-15 NKJV

166

"Blessed are the merciful: for they shall obtain mercy."

Matthew 5:7 KJV

Do not be overcome by evil, but overcome evil with good.

Romans 12:21

Be kind to each other, tenderhearted, forgiving one another, just as God through Christ has forgiven you.

Ephesians 4:32 NLT

Warm Reconciliation

Years after her experience in a Nazi concentration camp, Corrie ten Boom found herself standing face to face with one of the most cruel and heartless German guards she had met while in the camp. This man had humiliated and degraded both her and her sister.

Now he stood before her with an outstretched hand, asking, "Will you forgive me?"

Corrie said:

I stood there with coldness clutching at my heart, but I know that the will can function regardless of the temperature of the heart. I prayed, "Jesus, help me!" Woodenly, mechanically I thrust my hand into the one stretched out to me and I experienced an incredible thing. The current started in my shoulder, raced down into my arm, and sprang into our clutched hands. Then this warm reconciliation seemed to flood my whole being, bringing tears to my eyes. "I forgive you, brother," I cried with my whole heart. For a long moment we grasped each other's hands, the former guard, the former prisoner. I have never known the love of God so intensely as I did in that moment!

We learn the true meaning of mercy when it is given to us undeserved; and when we choose to extend mercy to others, God is faithful to soften our hearts with His great love. Raise your children to be mercy-givers, and they will discover that when they free others, they, themselves, are freed as well.

Reconciliation

The discretion of a man makes him slow to anger,
And his glory is to overlook a transgression.

Proverbs 19:11 NKJV

168

"Do not resist an evil person. If someone
strikes you on the right cheek, turn to him
the other also."

Matthew 5:39

"Whenever you stand praying, forgive, if you have
anything against any one; so that your Father also
who is in heaven may forgive you your trespasses."

Mark 11:25 RSV

"If thy brother trespass against thee, rebuke him;
and if he repent, forgive him."

Luke 17:3 KJV

Silence beyond Words

Marie Louise de La Ramee writes in *Ouida:* "There are many moments in friendship, as in love, when silence is beyond words. The faults of our friend may be clear to us, but it is well to seem to shut our eyes to them. Friendship is usually treated by the majority of mankind as a tough and everlasting thing which will survive all manner of bad treatment. But this is an exceedingly great and foolish error; it may die in an hour of a single unwise word."

If the words "I love you" are the most important three words, then the words "I'm sorry" are probably the *two* most important! Teach your children that when they are willing to admit fault, there is a greater likelihood that others will do the same. Instruct them to pursue peace in all their relationships, and remind them that being silent is sometimes the best option.

Restoration

Repent ye therefore, and be converted, that
your sins may be blotted out, when the times
of refreshing shall come from the presence of
the Lord.

Acts 3:19 KJV

170

Restore us, O God; make your face shine upon us,
that we may be saved.

Psalm 80:3

Cast away from you all your transgressions,
whereby ye have transgressed; and make you
a new heart and a new spirit.

Ezekiel 18:31 KJV

Turn to God! Give up your sins, and you will be
forgiven. Then that time will come when the Lord
will give you fresh strength.

Acts 3:19-20 CEV

Deciding When to Be Disturbed

A young family was moving to a new house. On moving day, Joe announced that an important meeting had been called at his new job, and he would be unable to help. Consequently, Jean had to handle the move by herself.

After the moving van came and left, she found herself standing in the living room of her new home. She was surrounded by boxes to be unpacked, appliances to be hooked up, a screaming baby, and a rambunctious five-year-old who had just decided to throw a metal toy truck through the picture window.

Fortunately nobody was hurt, but jagged glass fell everywhere, and a gale-force wind blew through the house. Jean felt she had to call Joe and tell him what had happened.

Joe's secretary informed her that he was in a meeting and couldn't be disturbed. "May I take a message?" the secretary asked.

"No, that's okay," Jean said, knowing Joe was notoriously lax about returning her calls. Then she said, "Wait, just tell him the insurance will cover everything."

The instant Joe got the message he called home.

It's wonderful to know God's forgiving love restores us, just as insurance restored the broken window. God never says, "I can't be disturbed" when we call on Him. May we treat our children with the same spirit!

Speech

Let your speech always be gracious, seasoned with salt, so that you may know how you ought to answer every one.

Colossians 4:6 RSV

172

The mouth of the righteous man utters wisdom, and his tongue speaks what is just.

Psalm 37:30

Whoso keepeth his mouth and his tongue keepeth his soul from troubles.

Proverbs 21:23 KJV

You must understand this, my beloved; let everyone be quick to listen, slow to speak, slow to anger.

James 1:19 NRSV

Wounds of the Heart

Many analogies have been given for the "untamed tongue." Francis Quarles likened it to a drawn sword that takes a person prisoner: "A word unspoken is like the sword in the scabbard, thine; if vented, thy sword is in another's hand."

Others have compared evil-speaking to the following things:

- A freezing wind—one that seals up the sparkling waters and kills the tender flowers and shoots of growth. In similar fashion, bitter and hate-filled words bind up the hearts of men and cause love to cease to flourish.
- A fox with a firebrand tied to its tail sent out among the standing corn just as in the days of Samson and the Philistines. So gossip spreads without control or reason.
- A pistol fired in the mountains, the echo of which is intensified until it sounds like thunder.

Perhaps the greatest analogy is one given by a little child who came running to her mother in tears. "Did your friend hurt you?" the mother asked.

"Yes," said the girl.

"Where?" asked her mother.

"Right here," said the child, pointing to her heart.

Words have the power to hurt and tear down your children or heal and uplift them. Ask God to help you place a guard on your tongue.[41]

Speech

A soft answer turns away wrath, but a harsh
word stirs up anger.

Proverbs 15:1 NRSV

174

But the tongue can no man tame; it is an unruly
evil, full of deadly poison.

James 3:8 KJV

How great a forest is set abalze by a small fire!
And the tongue is a fire.

James 3:5-6 NRSV

Let the words of my mouth, and the meditation
of my heart, be acceptable in thy sight, O LORD,
my strength, and my redeemer.

Psalm 19:14 KJV

It's Your Choice

Ida and David both wanted their sons to graduate from college. They knew their boys would have to pay their own way since David never made more than $150 a month. Still, they encouraged their sons to achieve all they could.

Arthur went directly from high school to a job. Edgar began studying law. When Dwight graduated high school, he didn't have a goal in mind, so he and Edgar made a pact: Dwight would work two years while Edgar studied, sending Edgar as much money as he could, and then they would reverse the arrangement. While working, Dwight found an opportunity that appealed to him more than college–West Point.

Both Ida and David were crushed by Dwight's decision. Ida was deeply convinced that soldiering was wicked. Still, all she ever said to him was, "It is your choice." David also remained silent, allowing his adult son full freedom to forge his own adult future. Yes, Ida and David wisely held their tongues–but they never withheld their applause, especially on the day their son, *General* Dwight Eisenhower, became president of the United States of America.

Refraining from giving advice may actually turn out to be the best gift you may ever give your child.[42]

Spiritual Growth

Let us stop going over the same old ground again and again, always teaching those first lessons about Christ. Let us go on instead to other things and become mature in our understanding, as strong Christians ought to be.

Hebrews 6:1 TLB

176

Practice these things and devote yourself to them, in order that your progress may be seen by all.

1 Timothy 4:15 TEV

Study to shew thyself approved unto God, a workman that needeth not to be ashamed, rightly dividing the word of truth.

2 Timothy 2:15 KJV

Open my eyes to see the wonderful truths in your law.

Psalm 119:18 NLT

The "Do Without" Club

Some teenage girls formed a "do without" club to raise money for missions. They determined to add to their fund by sacrificial giving. The majority of the girls were from well-to-do homes and easily found ways to contribute. Margie was different. Her family had little in the way of extras, and she found it extremely difficult to find something to contribute. One day she knelt by her bed and asked God to show her something she could do without. As she prayed, her pet spaniel licked her hands. Suddenly, she remembered that the family doctor had offered to buy him.

The tears came as she exclaimed, "Oh, Bright, I can't think of parting with you!" Then she thought of God's gift to the world. "I'll do it!" she said. Going to the doctor's home, she sold the dog for fifty dollars. Even though she missed her pet, she was still happy.

After learning of Margie's reason for selling her dog, the doctor returned him to her with a note attached to Bright's collar. It read: "Last night I offered what's left of my wasted life to God. I'd like to join your club and begin by doing without Bright."

Teach your children the value of sacrificial giving. It will not only cause them to grow stronger in their faith, but it also will have a tremendous impact on the people around them.[43]

Spiritual Growth

Put on all of God's armor so that you will be able to stand firm against all strategies and tricks of the Devil.

Ephesians 6:11 NLT

178

Grow in grace, and in the knowledge of our Lord and Saviour Jesus Christ. To him be glory both now and for ever. Amen.

2 Peter 3:18 KJV

The righteous man will flourish like the palm tree, He will grow like a cedar in Lebanon.

Psalm 92:12 NASB

This is my prayer: that your love may abound more and more in knowledge and depth of insight, so that you may be able to discern what is best and may be pure and blameless until the day of Christ.

Philippians 1:9-10

Deep Roots

Many people see abundant spring rains as a great blessing to farmers, especially if the rains come after the plants have sprouted and are several inches tall. What they don't realize is that even a short drought can have a devastating effect on a crop of seedlings that has received too much rain.

Why? Because during frequent rains, the young plants are not required to push their roots deeper into the soil in search of water. If a drought occurs later, plants with shallow root systems will quickly die.

We often receive abundance in our lives—rich fellowship, great teaching, thorough "soakings" of spiritual blessings. Yet when stress or tragedy enters our lives, we may find ourselves thinking God has abandoned us or is unfaithful. The fact is, we have allowed the "easiness" of our lives to keep us from pushing our spiritual roots deeper. We have allowed others to spoon-feed us, rather than develop our own deep personal relationship with God through prayer and study of His Word.

Teach your children that only the deeply rooted are able to endure hard times without wilting. The best advice for them is to enjoy the "rain" while seeking to grow even closer to Him.

Stewardship

He sat down opposite the treasury, and watched the multitude putting money into the treasury. Many rich people put in large sums. And a poor widow came, and put in two copper coins, which make a penny. And he called his disciples to him, and said to them, "Truly, I say to you, this poor widow has put in more than all those who are contributing to the treasury."

Mark 12:41-43 RSV

Command those who are rich in this present world not to be arrogant nor to put their hope in wealth, which is so uncertain, but to put their hope in God, who richly provides us with everything for our enjoyment. Command them to do good, to be rich in good deeds, and to be generous and willing to share.

1 Timothy 6:17-18

Although they were going through hard times and were very poor, they were glad to give generously. They gave as much as they could afford and even more, simply because they wanted to.

2 Corinthians 8:2-3 CEV

On every Lord's Day, each of you should put aside some amount of money in relation to what you have earned and save it for this offering. Don't wait until I get there and then try to collect it all at once.

1 Corinthians 16:2 NLT

Turning Pennies into Fortunes

Some years ago in Philadelphia, fifty-seven pennies were found under a little girl's pillow, pennies that left an unforgettable mark on the city.

The little girl attended what was called the Temple Sunday School. She, like many other children, joined her parents in supporting the expansion of the facilities by saving her pennies. Two years after she started her savings, the little girl became ill and died. Shortly after her death, her parents found a small purse under her pillow containing fifty-seven pennies and a piece of paper with the following delicately handwritten note: "To help build the Temple bigger, so more children can go to Sunday School."

The pastor told the story to the congregation, and the local newspaper featured it; soon her story had spread across the country. The pennies quickly grew into dollars, and the dollars into a huge fortune.

The outcome of the girl's seemingly insignificant effort can be seen in Philadelphia today. There is a church that will seat 3,000 persons and a college, Temple University, that is home to thousands of students, including famous alumnus Bill Cosby. Temple Hospital and Temple Sunday School are also located in this same city.

This is how stewardship works: Because one little girl gave what she could, millions were inspired to "go and do likewise." Teach your children this valuable lesson!

Stewardship

182

The Lord answered, "Who then is the faithful and wise manager, whom the master puts in charge of his servants to give them their food allowance at the proper time? It will be good for that servant whom the master finds doing so when he returns."

Luke 12:42-43

Now, a person who is put in charge as a manager must be faithful.

1 Corinthians 4:2 NLT

Each of you has been blessed with one of God's many wonderful gifts to be used in the service of others. So use your gift well.

1 Peter 4:10 CEV

Good will come to him who is generous and lends freely, who conducts his affairs with justice.

Psalm 112:5

Stewardship Starts in the Heart

Oseola McCarty practiced stewardship her entire life by helping people look nice. You see, she took in bundles of dirty clothes and washed and ironed them. She started after having to drop out of school in the sixth grade, and she carried out her work into her eighties.

Oseola never married, never had children. And for most of her eighty-seven years, Oseola McCarty spent almost no money. She lived in her old family home and wore simple clothes. She saved her money, most of it dollar bills and change, until she had amassed more than $150,000.

Then she made what people in Hattiesburg, Mississippi, are calling "The Gift." She donated her entire savings—all $150,000—to black college students across the state.

"I know it won't be too many years before I pass on," she explained, "and I wanted to share my wealth with the children."

Before her death, she was able to witness a number of "her children" graduate with the help of her financial support.

Raise your children to know that stewardship starts in the heart, and when their hearts are full of love and gratitude, they'll find a way to leave a legacy.

Strength

The LORD is my rock, and my fortress, and my deliverer; my God, my strength, in whom I will trust; my buckler, and the horn of my salvation, and my high tower.

Psalm 18:2 KJV

184

He gives strength to those who are tired and more power to those who are weak.

Isaiah 40:29 NCV

My soul melts from heaviness; Strengthen me according to Your word.

Psalm 119:28 NKJV

I have the strength to face all conditions by the power that Christ gives me.

Philippians 4:13 TEV

How Could It Be?

There were once two warring tribes in the Andes, one living in the lowlands and the other high in the mountains. One day the mountain people invaded the lowlanders, kidnapping a baby. They took the infant with them back up into the mountains.

The lowlanders didn't know how to climb the mountain or how to track the mountain people in the steep terrain. Even so, they sent out their best party of fighting men to climb the mountain and bring the baby home. After several days of striving, however, they had climbed only several hundred feet.

Feeling hopeless and helpless, the lowlander men decided that the cause was lost. As they prepared to return to their village below, they saw the baby's mother walking toward them. They realized that she was coming down the mountain that they hadn't figured out how to climb. And then they saw that she had the baby strapped to her back. How could that be?

One man greeted her and said, "We couldn't climb this mountain. How did you do this when we, the strongest and most able men in the village, couldn't do it?"

She shrugged her shoulders and said, "It wasn't your baby."

The bond between parents and their children is very strong indeed! Be sure to let your children see how valuable they are to you.[44]

Strength

In returning and rest shall ye be saved; in quietness
and in confidence shall be your strength.

Isaiah 30:15 KJV

186

I pray that out of his glorious riches he may
strengthen you with power through his Spirit in
your inner being, so that Christ may dwell in your
hearts through faith.

Ephesians 3:16-17

They that wait upon the Lord shall renew their
strength. They shall mount up with wings like
eagles; they shall run and not be weary; they
shall walk and not faint.

Isaiah 40:31 TLB

The LORD is my light and my salvation; whom
shall I fear? the LORD is the strength of my life;
of whom shall I be afraid?

Psalm 27:1 KJV

Licked from Within

In the novel *Gone with the Wind*, the prospective brother-in-law of Scarlett O'Hara gives this eulogy about her father:

"There warn't nothin' that come to him from the outside that could lick him. He warn't scared of the English government when they wanted to hang him. He just lit out and left home. And when he come to this country and was poor, that didn't scare him a mite neither. He went to work, and he made his money. And he warn't scared to tackle this section when it was part wild and the Injuns had just been run out of it. . . . And when the war come on and his money begun to go, he warn't scared to be poor again. And when the Yankees came through Tara and might of burnt him out or killed him, he warn't fazed a bit and he warn't licked neither."

And then facing the reality that O'Hara had died as a consequence of riding his horse while drunk, the eulogy ended,

"But he had . . . failin's, too, 'cause he could be licked from the inside. I mean to say that what the whole world couldn't do, his own heart could. . . . That weakness that's in our hearts can lick us in the time it takes to bat your eye."

Only God can transform inner weakness into strength. Ask Him to make you a better parent today.[45]

Stress

You will keep in perfect peace him whose mind is steadfast, because he trusts in you. Trust in the LORD forever, for the LORD, the LORD, is the Rock eternal.

Isaiah 26:3-4

188

The joy of the LORD is your strength.
Nehemiah 8:10 KJV

For unto us a child is born, unto us a son is given: and the government shall be upon his shoulder: and his name shall be called Wonderful, Counselor, The mighty God, The everlasting Father, The Prince of Peace.

Isaiah 9:6 KJV

Make music for him on harps. Play beautiful melodies! Sound the trumpets and horns and celebrate with joyful songs for our LORD and King! Command the ocean to roar with all of its creatures, and the earth to shout with all of its people.

Psalm 98:5-7 CEV

Stress Is No Match for Joy

Handel's masterpiece, *The Messiah,* has inspired millions through the centuries. Few know, however, that George Frederick Handel composed the lengthy oratorio in approximately three weeks. The music literally "came to him" in a flurry of notes and motifs. He composed feverishly, as if driven by the unseen Composer to put pen to paper. It is also little known that Handel composed the work while his eyesight was failing and while he was facing the threat of debtor's prison because of large, outstanding bills.

Most people find it difficult to create under stress, especially when physical or financial problems are the root of that stress, and yet, Handel found a way.

He credits the completion of the work to one thing: joy. He was quoted as saying that he felt as if his heart would burst with joy at what he was hearing in his mind and soul. It was that joy that compelled him to write, freed him to create, and ultimately found expression in the majestic "Hallelujah Chorus."

Handel lived to see his oratorio become a cherished tradition and a popular work. He was especially pleased to see it performed to raise money for benevolent causes—to help the less fortunate relieve the stress of life with joy.

Reduce the stress in your children's lives by instructing them to find joy in all they do. Remind them that God is creating unique masterpieces out of their lives, and encourage them to be filled with joy in the midst of this incredible journey.

Stress

Consider the blameless, observe the upright; there is a future for the man of peace.

Psalm 37:37

190

The peace of God, which passeth all understanding, shall keep your hearts and minds through Christ Jesus.

Philippians 4:7 KJV

"Come to Me, all you who labor and are heavy laden, and I will give you rest."

Matthew 11:28 NKJV

"I tell you to love your enemies and pray for anyone who mistreats you."

Matthew 5:44 CEV

Love Lasers

Claire Townsend worked in one of the most stressful workplaces—a major motion picture studio. She came to dread the daily morning meetings. New owners had taken control of the studio, jobs were uncertain, and, as a result, teamwork disappeared.

As she struggled with her stress, Claire paid more attention to her spiritual life. She began to pray again, and she rediscovered the power of God's love. Even so, the morning meetings exhausted her.

Then during a particularly tense meeting, a thought came to her: *Pray, pray, pray. Do it now.* As she did so, she felt God's love pulsating within her then radiating out like sunlight. She aimed a "love laser" toward the person who was making her feel the worst. This co-worker suddenly got quiet and eyed her curiously; Claire simply smiled back. One by one, she beamed God's love to each person around the table as she silently prayed.

Within minutes, the tone of the meeting completely changed. Compromise replaced confrontation. As the group relaxed, they became more creative and effective. From that day on, Claire looked forward to the meetings as an opportunity to share God's love.

Be sure your children are aware of the many benefits of prayer, including reduced stress and increased peace.

Success

It is very good if a man has received wealth from the Lord, and the good health to enjoy it. To enjoy your work and to accept your lot in life—that is indeed a gift from God.

Ecclesiastes 5:19 TLB

192

Riches and honor are with me, enduring wealth and prosperity. My fruit is better than gold, even fine gold, and my yield than choice silver.

Proverbs 8:18-19 RSV

The mind of man plans his way, But the LORD directs his steps.

Proverbs 16:9 NASB

Wealth and riches are in his house, and his righteousness endures forever.

Psalm 112:3

Doing Your Best

Cathy Rigby was a member of the U.S. Women's Gymnastics Team in the 1972 Olympics at Munich, and she had only one goal in mind—to win a gold medal. She had trained hard over a long period of time and knew she was ready to compete.

On the day she was scheduled to perform, she prayed for strength and the control to get through her routine without making mistakes. She was tense with determination not to let herself or the American team down.

She performed well, but when it was finished and the winners announced, her name was not among them. Cathy was crushed by her defeat. Afterward she joined her parents in the stands, all set for a good cry. As she sat down, she could barely manage to say, "I'm sorry. I did my best."

"You know that, and I know that," her mother said, "and I'm sure God knows that, too." Then Cathy recalls, her mother said ten words that she has never forgotten: "Doing your best is more important than being the best."

Help your kids understand that whether they win or lose, you still love them. In God's eyes, all of His children are winners![46]

Success

"I know the plans I have for you," declares the
LORD, "plans to prosper you and not to harm you,
plans to give you hope and a future."

Jeremiah 29:11

194

True humility and respect for the Lord lead a man
to riches, honor and long life.

Proverbs 22:4 TLB

They are like trees growing beside a stream, trees
that produce fruit in season and always have leaves.
Those people succeed in everything they do.

Psalm 1:3 CEV

Then the LORD your God will make you most
prosperous in all the work of your hands and in
the fruit of your womb, the young of your livestock
and the crops of your land.

Deuteronomy 30:9

Only One Move Needed

A ten-year-old boy decided to study judo despite the fact that he had lost his left arm in a devastating car accident. He began lessons with an old Japanese judo master. The boy couldn't understand why the master had taught him only one move.

"Sensei," the boy finally said, "shouldn't I be learning more moves?"

"This is the only move you know, but this is the only move you'll ever need to know," the *sensei* replied.

Several months later, the boy went to his first tournament. He deftly used his one move to win the first three matches and was now in the finals.

This time his opponent was more experienced. However, the other boy made a critical mistake: he dropped his guard. Instantly, the boy used his move to pin him. The boy had won the match and the tournament.

On the way home, the little boy asked, *"Sensei,* how did I win the tournament with only one move?"

"You won for two reasons," the *sensei* answered. "First, you've almost mastered one of the most difficult throws in all of judo. Second, the only known defense for that move is for your opponent to grip your left arm."

Are you teaching your children the skills they'll need to succeed in life?[47]

Thankfulness

196

Let your roots grow down into him and draw up
nourishment from him. See that you go on
growing in the Lord, and become strong and
vigorous in the truth you were taught. Let your
lives overflow with joy and thanksgiving for all
he has done.

Colossians 2:7 TLB

Whatever you do or say, let it be as a representative
of the Lord Jesus, and come with him into
the presence of God the Father to give him
your thanks.

Colossians 3:17 TLB

Thanks be to God, who gives us the victory
through our Lord Jesus Christ.

1 Corinthians 15:57 NASB

Give thanks in all circumstances, for this is God's
will for you in Christ Jesus.

1 Thessalonians 5:18

An Attitude of Gratitude

Fulton Oursler told a story of an old nurse who was born a slave on the eastern shore of Maryland. She had not only attended Fulton's birth, but also that of his mother. He credits her for teaching him the greatest lesson he ever learned about thankfulness and contentment. Recalls Oursler:

> I remember her as she sat at the kitchen table in our house—the hard, old, brown hands folded across her starched apron; the glistening eyes; and the husky old whispering voice, saying, "Much obliged, Lord, for my vittles."
>
>
> "Anna," I asked, "what's a vittle?"
>
> "It's what I've got to eat and drink—that's vittles," the old nurse replied.
>
> "But you'd get your vittles whether you thanked the Lord or not."
>
> "Sure," said Anna, "but it makes everything taste better to be thankful."

For many people, poverty is not a condition of the pocketbook, but a state of mind. How do your children view themselves today? Do they think of themselves as being rich or poor? What do they value and count as "wealth" in their lives? Train them to be thankful for what they have, and then they will be very wealthy indeed!

Thankfulness

Give thanks to the LORD, for he is good; his love endures forever. Let them give thanks to the LORD for his unfailing love and his wonderful deeds for men. Let them sacrifice thank offerings and tell of his works with songs of joy.

198

Psalm 107:1,21-22

The LORD is my strength and my shield; my heart trusts in him, and I am helped. My heart leaps for joy and I will give thanks to him in song.

Psalm 28:7

Then he turned my sorrow into joy! He took away my clothes of mourning and clothed me with joy so that I might sing glad praises to the Lord. . . . O Lord my God, I will keep on thanking you forever!

Psalm 30:11-12 TLB

Come, let us sing for joy to the LORD, Let us shout joyfully to the rock of our salvation. Let us come before His presence with thanksgiving, Let us shout joyfully to Him with psalms.

Psalm 95:1-2 NASB

Thou Shalt Not Whine

Teach your children the following four steps for turning whining into thanksgiving:

1. *Give something away.* When you give, you create both a physical and a mental space for something new and better to come into your life. Although you may think you are "lacking" something in life, when you give, you demonstrate the abundance you have.

2. *Narrow your goals.* Don't expect everything good to come into your life all at once. When you focus your expectations toward specific, attainable goals, you are more apt to direct your time and energy toward reaching them.

3. *Change your vocabulary from "I need" to "I want."* Most of the things you think you *need* are actually things you *want.* If you change your thinking, you will be thankful for even small luxuries when you receive them, rather than seeing them as necessities you can't live without.

4. *Choose to be thankful for what you already have.* Thanksgiving is a choice. We all have more things to be thankful for than we could even begin to recount in a single day.

As your children put these steps into practice, they will find themselves whining less and thanking God more. They will learn that living a life of gratitude and thanksgiving to God is the best antidote for stress!

Trust

It is better to take refuge in the LORD than
to trust in man.

Psalm 118:8

200

You will keep in perfect peace him whose mind
is steadfast, because he trusts in you. Trust in
the LORD forever, for the LORD, the LORD, is
the Rock eternal.

Isaiah 26:3-4

Blessed is the man who trusts in the LORD,
whose confidence is in him.

Jeremiah 17:7

"Trust in God; trust also in me."

John 14:1

My Father's Hands

A crew of botanists was searching in the Alps for rare flowers. A very fine specimen was spotted on a small ledge of rock that could only be reached with a lifeline. The job was far too dangerous for the inexperienced botanists, so they called in a local shepherd boy who was familiar with the region. They offered him several gold coins to climb down the rope and recover the rare flower.

Although the boy desperately wanted the coins, he feared that the task was too risky. Several times he peered over the edge of the cliff, but he couldn't see any safe way of getting to the flower. Besides, he would have to place his life in the hands of the strangers who would be holding his lifeline. Then the boy had an idea. He left the group for a few moments and finally returned, holding the hand of a much older man. The shepherd boy then ran eagerly to the brink of the cliff and said to the botanists, "You can tie the rope under my arms now. I'll go into the canyon, as long as you let my father hold the rope."

This boy shared a trusting relationship with his father and was willing to put his life into his father's hands.

In the same way that your children trust in you, put your trust in your Heavenly Father today.[48]

Trust

Blessed is the man who makes the LORD his trust,
who does not look to the proud, to those who
turn aside to false gods.

Psalm 40:4

202

This is what the Sovereign LORD, the Holy One
of Israel, says: "In repentance and rest is your
salvation, in quietness and trust is your strength."

Isaiah 30:15

This is what the Sovereign LORD says: "See,
I lay a stone in Zion, a tested stone, a precious
cornerstone for a sure foundation; the one who
trusts will never be dismayed."

Isaiah 28:16

When I am afraid, I will trust in you.

Psalm 56:3

Nursing a Splinter

One afternoon while playing on a wooden picnic table, a little boy ran a splinter into his finger. Sobbing, he called his father, who was a pastor, at his office. He said, "Daddy, I want God to take the splinter out."

The father said, "Go to your mother. She'll be able to remove it for you."

"No," the little boy insisted, "I want God to take it out."

"Why don't you trust your mother to do it?" his father asked.

"Because when Mommy takes a splinter out, it hurts. If God takes it out, it won't hurt."

When the father arrived home at the end of his workday, he found his son still nursing a sore and inflamed finger. In spite of his son's initial protests, the father proceeded to remove the splinter. The procedure was a bit painful, but the relief was complete.

Somehow, this little boy had gotten the impression that God's healing was painless and would not hurt him. Unfortunately, the healing process can be painful, so teach your children to trust God regardless of the pain. Teach them, too, that God often involves others in the healing process: parents, doctors, ministers, and counselors, just to name a few.[49]

Truth

Surely you heard of him and were taught in him in accordance with the truth that is in Jesus.

Ephesians 4:21

204

All Scripture is inspired by God and is useful for teaching the truth, rebuking error, correcting faults, and giving instruction for right living.

2 Timothy 3:16 TEV

The words of the LORD are flawless, like silver refined in a furnace of clay, purified seven times.

Psalm 12:6

The LORD hates . . . A proud look, A lying tongue, Hands that shed innocent blood.

Proverbs 6:16-17 NKJV

The Missing Chapter

One Sunday morning, a minister announced to his congregation that the topic for the next Sunday's sermon would be "integrity." In preparation, he asked them to study the wisdom of Solomon found in Proverbs 32.

The minister began the service the next Sunday by asking the congregation how many had read the assigned scripture. Several hands were raised when the question was asked.

"Just as I thought," said the minister, "there is no thirty-second chapter in the book of Proverbs. Thereby, the need for this sermon on honesty."

One of the first lessons parents usually teach their preschoolers is: "Thou shalt not tell a lie." We expect our children to tell us the truth whatever the circumstances. In return we should model the same behavior. Too many times parents excuse their behavior by making excuses: "It's just a little white lie; they wouldn't understand."

Children understand when someone isn't being truthful with them. It's not necessary to give them a long explanation and go into all the details that they probably wouldn't be able to understand, but it is possible to give them an age-appropriate and truthful answer.[50]

Truth

Do not testify falsely against your neighbor.

Exodus 20:16 NLT

206

We will lovingly follow the truth at all times—
speaking truly, dealing truly, living truly—and so
become more and more in every way like Christ.

Ephesians 4:15-16 TLB

[Jesus said]: "This is why I was born and came
into the world: to tell people the truth. And
everyone who belongs to the truth listens to me."

John 18:37 NCV

Now, O Lord GOD, You are God, and Your
words are truth.

2 Samuel 7:28 NASB

The Spilled Feathers

*J*ealous of the mayor's election victory, the wife of his opponent spread malicious lies about the mayor throughout the town. The rumors and gossip brought the life of the mayor under scrutiny, and although he had done nothing of which to be ashamed, he resigned, feeling it was impossible to continue in office without the respect of those he served.

Later, overcome with remorse, the woman went to the ex-mayor to beg his forgiveness. "Please tell me, how can I make amends?" she said. "I'll do anything you say."

The man replied, "Open a goose-down pillow, and allow the feathers to spill to the ground."

She nodded, "And then what?"

He said, "Wait ten minutes, and then pick up all the feathers."

The woman returned the next day with only a small portion of the feathers in the ripped-open pillow case. "How did you do?" he asked.

She answered, "The feathers blew everywhere, and I was unable to retrieve them all."

He said soberly, "Rumors and gossip are equally impossible to retrieve."

Teach your children that what they say about people has far-reaching, ripple effects. Teach them to make certain that what they say is, not only true, but that it needs saying.[51]

Wisdom

The LORD grants wisdom! From his mouth come knowledge and understanding.

Proverbs 2:6 NLT

208

I will praise the LORD, who counsels me; even at night my heart instructs me.

Psalm 16:7

God has chosen the foolish things of the world to shame the wise, and God has chosen the weak things of the world to shame the things which are strong.

1 Corinthians 1:27 NASB

The foolishness of God is wiser than men, and the weakness of God is stronger than men.

1 Corinthians 1:25 RSV

Life Buoys

Sara Orne Jewett has written a beautiful novel about Maine, *The Country of the Pointed Firs.* In it, she describes the path that leads a woman writer from her home to that of a retired sea captain named Elijah Tilley. On the way, there are a number of wooden stakes in the ground that appear to be randomly scattered on his property. Each is painted white and trimmed in yellow, just like the captain's house.

Once she arrives at the captain's abode, she asks him what the stakes mean. He tells her that when he first made the transition from sailing the seas to plowing the land, he discovered his plow would catch on many of the large rocks just beneath the surface of the ground. Recalling how buoys in the sea always marked trouble spots for him, he set out the stakes as "land buoys" to mark the rocks. Then he could avoid plowing over them in the future.

God's promises and commandments are like buoys for you and your children, revealing the trouble spots and rocky points of life. When you follow the wisdom found in God's Word and thereby steer clear of what is harmful to you, life is not only more enjoyable, but more productive.

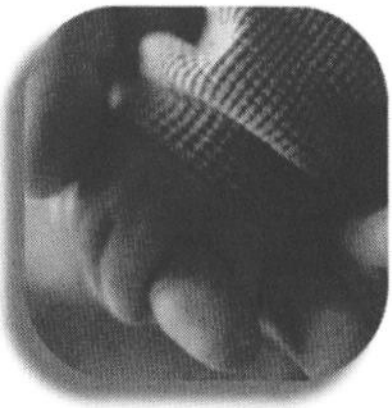

Wisdom

You desire honesty from the heart, so you can teach me to be wise in my inmost being.

Psalm 51:6 NLT

The fear of the LORD is the beginning of wisdom; all who follow his precepts have good understanding. To him belongs eternal praise.

Psalm 111:10

O that ye would altogether hold your peace! and it should be your wisdom.

Job 13:5 KJV

Wisdom calls aloud outside; She raises her voice in the open squares.

Proverbs 1:20 NKJV

Hard of Heeding

Jed Harris, the producer of *Our Town* and numerous other plays, became convinced he was losing his hearing. He went to one physician who couldn't find anything wrong, so he referred Harris to a specialist.

The specialist gave him a thorough checkup, and nothing showed up to indicate a technical problem with his hearing. The doctor finally pulled a gold watch out of his pocket and asked, "Can you hear this ticking?"

Harris said, "Of course."

The specialist walked a few feet away and held up the watch again. "Now can you hear it?" he asked.

Harris concentrated and answered, "Yes, I can still hear it clearly."

Finally the doctor walked out the door of the examining room into the hallway and called, "Can you hear it now?"

Again, he said, "Yes."

The specialist came back into the room and announced, "Mr. Harris, there is nothing wrong with your hearing. You just don't listen."

Sometimes the rush and distraction of our life renders us temporarily deaf to the wisdom that is available all around us. Our children, for example, are discovering the truths of life every day, and we might be amazed at what we can learn from them—when we listen.

Work

Work hard and cheerfully at all you do, just as though you were working for the Lord and not merely for your masters, remembering that it is the Lord Christ who is going to pay you, giving you your full portion of all he owns. He is the one you are really working for.

Colossians 3:23-24 TLB

212

When God gives any man wealth and possessions, and enables him to enjoy them, to accept his lot and be happy in his work—this is a gift of God.

Ecclesiastes 5:19

"Don't work for food that spoils. Work for food that gives eternal life. The Son of Man will give you this food, because God the Father has given him the right to do so."

John 6:27 CEV

God is not unfair. He will not forget how hard you have worked for him and how you have shown your love to him by caring for other Christians, as you still do.

Hebrews 6:10 NLT

A Difficult Decision

In *New Man* magazine, Gary Oliver writes about a difficult decision made by professional baseball player Tim Burke:

> While working as a successful pitcher for the Montreal Expos, Tim and his wife wanted to start a family but discovered they were unable to have children. After much prayer, they decided to adopt four special-needs children. This led to one of the most difficult decisions of Tim's life.
>
> The successful baseball player discovered that his life on the road conflicted with his ability to be a quality husband and father. After much prayer and soul-searching, Tim made what many considered an unbelievable decision: he decided to give up professional baseball.
>
> When Tim left the stadium for the last time, reporters wanted to know why he was retiring. "Baseball is going to do just fine without me," he said. "It's not going to miss a beat. But I'm the only father my children have. I'm the only husband my wife has. And they need me a lot more than baseball does."

It's important to be available to your children to help them make the little everyday decisions of life. Then as they grow up, you can have confidence about how they'll handle the bigger ones.[52]

Work

Six days shall work be done: but the seventh day *is* the sabbath of rest, and holy convocation; ye shall do no work therein: it *is* the sabbath of the LORD in all your dwellings.

Leviticus 23:3 KJV

Each man's work will become evident; for the day will show it, because it is to be revealed with fire; and the fire itself will test the quality of each man's work.

I Corinthians 3:13 NASB

God has promised us a Sabbath when we will rest, even though it has not yet come. On that day God's people will rest from their work, just as God rested from his work.

Hebrews 4:9-10 CEV

Even when we were with you, we gave you this rule: "If a man will not work, he shall not eat."

2 Thessalonians 3:10

A Date for the Circus

The two boys were dressed and ready to go. Excitement flooded their faces and all their talk was about only one thing: their father had promised to take them to the circus that afternoon!

Dad came home from work after lunch and quickly changed into casual clothing. Just as the three of them were about to leave the house, the phone rang. The boys listened as their father talked with the person on the other end of the line. Bit by bit, their faces began to fall. This was obviously a business call. Disappointment rolled into the room like a dark cloud. Their mother also overheard what she thought was the inevitable change of plans. Then to everyone's surprise, they heard Dad say, "No, I won't be down. It will just have to wait until morning."

He hung up the phone and called for the boys to meet him at the car. As he turned to kiss his wife goodbye, she smiled, and with a tinge of fear that he may have made the wrong decision, she said, "The circus keeps coming back, you know."

Her husband replied, "Yes, I know, but childhood doesn't."

Time goes so quickly. Enjoy your children today.[53]

Worship

Therefore, I urge you, brothers, in view of God's mercy, to offer your bodies as living sacrifices, holy and pleasing to God—this is your spiritual act of worship.

Romans 12:1

216

God bought you with a high price. So you must honor God with your body.

1 Corinthians 6:20 NLT

Spread for me a banquet of praise, serve High God a feast of kept promises.

Psalm 50:15 THE MESSAGE

I will praise you, O Lord my God, with all my heart; I will glorify your name forever.

Psalm 86:12

Autumn Dance

In *Mothering by Heart,* Robin Jones Gunn writes of this example of unashamed worship of our Creator:

> She stood a short distance from her guardian at the park this afternoon, her distinctive features revealing that although her body blossomed into young adulthood, her mind would always remain a child's. My children ran and jumped and sifted sand through perfect, coordinated fingers. Caught up in fighting over a shovel, they didn't notice when the wind changed. But she did. A wild autumn wind spinning leaves into amber flurries.
>
>
> I called to my boisterous son and jostled my daughter. Time to go. . . . My rosy-cheeked boy stood tall, watching with wide-eyed fascination the gyrating dance of the Down's syndrome girl as she scooped up leaves and showered herself with a twirling rain of autumn jubilation.
>
> With each twist and hop she sang deep, earthy grunts—a canticle of praise meant only for the One whose breath causes the leaves to tremble from the trees.
>
> Hurry up. Let's go. Seat belts on? I start the car. In the rearview mirror I study her one more time through misty eyes. And then the tears come. Not tears of pity for her. The tears are for me. For I am far too sophisticated to publicly shout praises to my Creator.

Train your children to boldly worship their Creator! Take time, together, each day to truly praise Him and to thank Him for His many blessings.

Worship

"Let your good deeds shine out for all to see, so that everyone will praise your heavenly Father."
Matthew 5:16 NLT

218

Whatever you do, work at it with all your heart, as working for the Lord, not for men.
Colossians 3:23

Whatever you do or say, let it be as a representative of the Lord Jesus, all the while giving thanks through him to God the Father.
Colossians 3:17 NLT

Shout Hallelujah, you God-worshipers; give glory, you sons of Jacob; adore him, you daughters of Israel. He has never let you down, never looked the other way when you were being kicked around.
Psalm 22:23-24 THE MESSAGE

Worship and Worry

Ruth Bell Graham tells the story of when God taught her that worship is the antidote for worry. She was in a foreign country, wide-awake at 3 A.M., so she began to pray for one who was running away from God. She says, "When it is dark and the imagination runs wild, there are fears only a mother can understand."

Then suddenly, the Lord told her to "quit studying the problem and start studying the promises." So she opened her Bible and began to read Philippians 4:6 KJV: "Be careful for nothing; but in everything by prayer and supplication *with thanksgiving. . . .*" She recalls:

> Suddenly I realized the missing ingredient in my prayers had been "with thanksgiving." So I put down my Bible and spent time worshiping Him for Who and What He is. This covers more territory than any one mortal can comprehend. Even contemplating what little we do know dissolves doubts, reinforces faith, and restores joy. It was as if someone turned on the lights in my mind and heart, and the little fears and worries that had been nibbling away in the darkness like mice and cockroaches hurriedly scuttled for cover. That was when I learned that worship and worry cannot live in the same heart: they are mutually exclusive.

As a parent, you are presented daily with challenges and situations that can be worrisome. Choose to turn those cares over to the Lord and worship Him instead. Praise Him for His faithfulness, and trust Him to provide the answers and solutions that you need.

219

Endnotes

1   (p. 9) Craig Larson, *Choice Contemporary Stories and Illustrations for Preachers, Teachers, and Writers* (Grand Rapids, Michigan: Baker Books, 1998) p. 13.

2   (p. 27) *Encyclopedia of 7700 Illustrations,* Paul Lee Tan, editor (Dallas, Texas: Bible Communications, 1979) p. 1008.

3   (p. 35) *God's Little Devotional Book for Dads* (Tulsa, Oklahoma: Honor Books, 1995) p. 47.

4   (p. 41) "Heroes for Today" column, *Reader's Digest* (June 1997) pp. 99-100.

5   (p. 49) Roy B. Zuck, *The Speaker's Quote Book* (Grand Rapids, Michigan: Kregel Publications, 1997) p. 49.

6   (p. 57) *Look for the Rainbow,* Christian internet site online at www.nytimes.com, 1999.

7   (p. 59) *1100 Illustrations from the Writings of D. L. Moody,* John Reed, editor (Grand Rapids, Michigan: Baker Book House, 1996) p. 247.

8   (p. 61) Roy B. Zuck, *The Speaker's Quote Book* (Grand Rapids, Michigan: Kregel Publications, 1997) p. 262.

9   (p. 63) *Top 100 Inspirational Anecdotes and Wisdom* (part 5), online at www.bizmove.com/inspiration, 1999, p. 7.

10 (p. 67) John Croyle, *Parent's Place, Love Unconditionally,* online at www.focusonthefamily.com, 1999, pp. 1-2.

11 (p. 69) Roy B. Zuck, *The Speaker's Quote Book* (Grand Rapids, Michigan: Kregel Publications, 1997) pp. 51-52.

12 (p. 71) Craig Larson, *Choice Contemporary Stories and Illustrations for Preachers, Teachers, and Writers* (Grand Rapids, Michigan: Baker Books, 1998) p. 34.

13 (p. 73) W. B. Freeman, *God's Little Lessons on Life for Mom* (Tulsa, Oklahoma: Honor Books, 1999) p. 63.

14 (p. 79) *1100 Illustrations from the Writings of D. L. Moody,* John W. Reed, editor (Grand Rapids, Michigan: Baker Book House, 1996) p. 18.

15 (p. 89) Roy B. Zuck, *The Speaker's Quote Book* (Grand Rapids, Michigan: Kregel Publications, 1997) p. 237.

16 (p. 91) *God's Little Devotional Book* (Tulsa, Oklahoma: Honor Books, 1998) p. 127.

17 (p. 93) W. B. Freeman, *God's Little Lessons on Life for Mom* (Tulsa, Oklahoma: Honor Books, 1999) p. 170.

18 (p. 99) W. B. Freeman, *God's Little Lessons on Life for Mom* (Tulsa, Oklahoma: Honor Books, 1999) p. 30.

19 (p. 105) James S. Hewett, *Illustrations Unlimited* (Wheaton, Illinois: Tyndale House Publishers, 1988) p. 235.

20 (p. 111) Roy B. Zuck, *The Speaker's Quote Book* (Grand Rapids, Michigan: Kregel Publications, 1997) pp. 236-237.

21 (p. 113) *God's Little Devotional Book for Dads* (Tulsa, Oklahoma: Honor Books, 1995) p. 159.

22 (p. 119) Roy B. Zuck, *The Speaker's Quote Book* (Grand Rapids, Michigan: Kregel Publications, 1997) p. 239.

23 (p. 121) *God's Little Devotional Book for Dads* (Tulsa, Oklahoma: Honor Books, 1995) p. 173.

24 (p. 123) *Like a Child, Christian Fellowship Devotionals,* found online at www.cfdevotionals.org, August 5, 1999.

25 (p. 125) Jacob Braude, *Braudes Treasury of Wit & Humor for All Occasions* (Paramus, New Jersey: Prentice Hall, 1991) p. 139.

26 (p. 127) Claire Cloninger, *A Childlike Heart, Women's Devotional Bible #2,* NIV (Grand Rapids, Michigan: Zondervan Publishing House, 1995) p. 519.

27   (p. 129) George Sweeting, *Who Said That* (Chicago, Illinois: Moody Press, 1995) pp. 247-248.

28   (p. 131) Roy B. Zuck, *The Speaker's Quote Book* (Grand Rapids, Michigan: Kregel Publications, 1997) pp. 234,236.

29   (p. 133) W. B. Freeman, *God's Little Lessons on Life for Mom* (Tulsa, Oklahoma: Honor Books, 1999) p. 45.

30   (p. 141) Herbert Prochnow, *Treasury of Inspiration* (Grand Rapids, Michigan: Baker Book House, 1958) p. 20.

31   (p. 147) Philippe, *Just for Parents*, online at www.members.xoom.com/XMCM/BouBou/pr/parents8.htm, 1999, p. 8.

32   (p. 149) Craig Larson, *Choice Contemporary Stories and Illustrations for Preachers, Teachers, and Writers* (Grand Rapids, Michigan: Baker Books, 1998) p. 47.

33   (p. 151) *God's Little Devotional Book for Dads* (Tulsa, Oklahoma: Honor Books, 1995) p. 69.

34   (p. 153) W. B. Freeman, *God's Little Lessons on Life for Mom* (Tulsa, Oklahoma: Honor Books, 1999) p. 95.

35   (p. 155) Herbert Prochnow, *Treasury of Inspiration* (Grand Rapids, Michigan: Baker Book House, 1958) p. 21.

36   (p. 157) *God's Little Devotional Book for Dads* (Tulsa, Oklahoma: Honor Books, 1995) p. 33.

37   (p. 159) *God's Little Devotional Book for Dads* (Tulsa, Oklahoma: Honor Books, 1995) p. 29.

38   (p. 161) Herbert Prochnow, *Treasury of Inspiration* (Grand Rapids, Michigan: Baker Book House, 1958) p. 86.

39   (p. 163) W. B. Freeman, *Sunset with God* (Tulsa, Oklahoma: Honor Books, 1999) pp. 138-139.

40   (p. 165) W. B. Freeman, *God's Little Lessons on Life for Mom* (Tulsa, Oklahoma: Honor Books, 1999) p. 163.

41   (p. 173) W. B. Freeman, *God's Little Lessons on Life for Mom* (Tulsa, Oklahoma: Honor Books, 1999) p. 83.

42   (p. 175) Roy B. Zuck, *The Speaker's Quote Book* (Grand Rapids, Michigan: Kregel Publications, 1997) p.165.

43   (p. 177) *Top 100 Inspirational Anecdotes and Wisdom* (part 4), found online at www.bizmove.com/inspiration, 1999, pp. 4-5.

44   (p. 185) Glenn Van Ekeren, *Words for All Occasions* (Paramus, New Jersey: Prentice Hall, 1988) pp. 65-66.

45   (p. 187) Roy B. Zuck, *The Speaker's Quote Book* (Grand Rapids, Michigan: Kregel Publications, 1997) p. 147.

46   (p. 193) *Top 100 Inspirational Anecdotes and Wisdom* (part 4), found online at www.bizmove.com/inspiration, 1999, p. 2.

47   (p. 195) Kathy Collard Miller and D. Larry Miller, *God's Vitamin C for the Spirit* (Lancaster, Pennsylvania: Starburst Publishers, 1996) p. 64.

48   (p. 201) J. Dargatz, *God Will Make a Way* (Tulsa, Oklahoma: Albury Publishing, 1999) pp. 156-157.

49   (p. 203) Jacob Braude, *Braudes Treasury of Wit & Humor for all Occasions* (Paramus, New Jersey: Prentice Hall, 1991) p. 94.

50   (p. 205) Glenn Van Ekeren, *Words for All Occasions* (Paramus, New Jersey: Prentice Hall, 1988) pp. 88-89.

51   (p. 207) Craig Larson, *Choice Contemporary Stories and Illustrations for Preachers, Teachers, and Writers* (Grand Rapids, Michigan: Baker Books, 1998) p. 85.

52   (p. 213) *God's Little Devotional Book for Dads* (Tulsa, Oklahoma: Honor Books, 1995) p. 49.

53   (p. 215) W. B. Freeman, *God's Little Lessons on Life for Mom* (Tulsa, Oklahoma: Honor Books, 1999) p. 96.

Additional copies of this book
and other titles from Honor Books
are available from your local bookstore.

God's Little Lessons on Life
God's Little Lessons on Life for Dad
God's Little Lessons on Life for Graduates
God's Little Lessons on Life for Mom
God's Little Lessons for Leaders
God's Little Lessons for Teachers
God's Little Lessons for Teens

If you have enjoyed this book,
or if it has impacted your life,
we would like to hear from you.

Please contact us at:

Honor Books
Department E
P.O. Box 55388
Tulsa, Oklahoma 74155
Or by e-mail at info@honorbooks.com